The Rise of the

INDIAN ROPE
TRICK

The Rise of the

INDIAN ROPE TRICK

*How a Spectacular Hoax
Became History*

PETER LAMONT

THUNDER'S MOUTH PRESS
NEW YORK

THE RISE OF THE INDIAN ROPE TRICK
How a Spectacular Hoax Became History

Published by
Thunder's Mouth Press
An Imprint of Avalon Publishing Group Inc.
245 West 17th St., 11th Floor
New York, NY 10011

AVALON
publishing group incorporated

Library of Congress Cataloging-in-Publication Data is available.

ISBN 1-56025-661-3

9   8   7   6   5   4   3   2   1

Book design by M Rules
Printed in the United States of America
Distributed by Publishers Group West

*To my parents
who never read my doctoral thesis*

CONTENTS

ACKNOWLEDGEMENTS

It all began quietly enough in the National Library of Scotland, reading a Victorian edition of Marco Polo's travels. It is very quiet in the library. Nobody dares cough for fear of being heckled by a frenzy of tut-tuts in educated Edinburgh accents. And it was in the midst of that tense silence that I came across a footnote, a footnote that started me wondering whether the legend of the Indian rope trick had been around for as long as everybody thought. Five years later, I finished the book. I am referring, of course, to this book, not the Victorian edition of Marco Polo's travels. I still intend to finish that book, as soon as my sore throat has cleared up.

It was later in London that Dr Richard Wiseman got involved. Between us, Richard and I collected reams of evidence in a bid to discover what the witnesses really saw, we presented papers at conferences together, and we co-published a couple of articles. If one of us gave a radio or television interview, the other was there. When I travelled to India in the hope of seeing the rope trick performed, Richard was with me. I began to wonder whether I would ever get rid of him. But finally he left, to go in search of the world's funniest joke, and I shudder to think what else. I would say that I miss him, but the fact is that I just got off the phone with him. He called about another project. And I have no idea how he found my new number.

In the search for evidence, there were many weird and wonderful possessors of strange stuff who helped. There was Alan Wesencraft, then curator of the Harry Price Collection at the University of London, who would hand you the most esoteric book before you had finished saying its title. There was Professor Marcello Truzzi, whose breadth of knowledge about all things bizarre was, at times, genuinely scary.* There was Peter Lane, librarian of the Magic Circle, who would constantly interrupt my work with another rare newspaper article he had discovered in his files. Quite frankly, that became a little annoying. And Professor Eddie Dawes, who (and this has been scientifically demonstrated) knows everything about the history of magic. And, of course, Professor Eberhard Bauer, who would dig up articles in German, and translate the relevant passages for those of us

---

* Marcello died between completion of the manuscript and publication. Though we never met, his support and advice were invaluable. I would love to have known what he thought of the book.

who remain Anglocentric monolinguists. Which, I think, is just showing off.

Other gems were supplied by Mark Pilkington of *Fortean Times*, and Douglas Cameron of Glasgow Magic Circle (just a wee joke, Douglas). At the University of Edinburgh, there were Professor Rhodri Jeffreys-Jones and Dr Crispin Bates at the History department, and Paul Dundas of the Sanskrit department. All of which might make you wonder whether I actually found out anything myself. But if I had not, I would never have had to rely on the staff of the libraries of Edinburgh University, the Magic Circle, the Indian Institute, and the Society for Psychical Research, as well as the National Library of Scotland and the British Library (which is also very quiet). Later, and nobody predicted this, I needed Mike Samson at the United States Secret Service archives, who must know some very interesting stuff, though he quite properly kept to the topic in hand. To say that this book could not have been written without any of them is a cliché and, in any case, it is untrue, but it certainly would have been shorter.

But information is only part of the story, for there are two more things you need if you are to write a book of this sort. The first is time off work, which seems like a good point to thank my boss, Professor Bob Morris (is there ever a bad time to thank your boss?). And then you need to think the book will work, which means (in my case at least) that you need others to tell you it will work. It was Peter Tallack at Orion who first suggested it. Then Jon Ronson, whom I met at a Festival of Lying, told me it was a great idea, and I believed him. So I contacted Sam Boyce, who became my agent, and she sounded so excited I knew it could work. I later discovered she always sounds excited, but that's why she's a wee gem. And Claudia, yes Claudia, who regularly told me how good it was, always with a straight face, and who virtually insisted that I go to India to write the book. I could easily have taken that the wrong way, had she not insisted that she come along for a bit as well. Cheeky monkey.

In India, I was sustained by my pal, Geoff, who was living his own weird story at the time. And by Raju, with whom I stayed, and who refused to let me mention him or his guest house unless he got a commission (acknowledgements don't count, Raju). And by Sham, who does the worst Scottish accent since Mel Gibson, and Arun, who cheats at Karum, but is otherwise an all-round good guy. And by Professor Shankar and his family, who organised, hosted and performed during two wonderful conventions of Indian magic. And when I got back, Tim Whiting demonstrated admirable taste by becoming my editor, and gave me sound advice along the rest of the way, even if he couldn't provide chicken nuggets at the posh Time Warner lunch. And no doubt many others helped too, but I suspect the only people continuing to read this are those who expect to be mentioned and have not been mentioned yet. Boy, are you going to be disappointed. But I have not forgotten your contribution. I am merely recognising that you are above such petty praise, and that you need only know I appreciate your help. Well, I do. Thank you. You know who you are.

AUTHOR'S NOTE (FOR THE DISCERNING READER ONLY)

Few people will read this. At least the Acknowledgements will be read by those who were thanked, and by those who thought they were going to be thanked. This latter group, now bitter and resentful at having apparently been forgotten, will waste no more time on the preliminaries, while the former group, now smug with recognition, will carelessly flick past these pages en route to the story they now feel partially responsible for. Few indeed will venture here, so the fact that you are reading this makes you special. It also automatically suggests that you are the sort of person who should read this, who will get the most from it, and that makes you fortunate as well as special. You are clearly a thorough person, someone who takes little for granted, and that sort of scepticism is not only healthy but admirable. Unfortunately, it also means you are unlikely to be swayed by superficial praise such as this, so perhaps we should move on to the mildly amusing but relevant anecdote.

*

It was many years ago that I first became interested in history, though it was not until I had left school. In my youthful arrogance, the first book I decided to buy was a copy of *The History of the World* by J. M. Roberts. I figured that, after reading it, I would know about the history of the world. A few pages in, however, it became clear that this was going to be a very long story. And so I turned to the index and looked up my home country of Scotland, thinking it best to begin with something more familiar to me than the emergence of *Homo sapiens*. I was devastated to discover that Scotland barely got a mention. Scottish history amounted to: the Vikings had pillaged it, it had fought with England, and it had been backward until the 'intellectual flowering' of the Enlightenment. And, according to the index to the history of the world, my home town of Edinburgh did not even exist. I decided never to trust a historian again. Since that dreadful loss of innocence, I have read hundreds of history books, I have become an academic historian myself, and some of my closest friends are historians, but I still don't trust them. Perhaps I should explain why.

There is some confusion about what history is. It is not the past, though it is about the past. It is, some say, a narrative based on historical facts – but which facts? After all, the past has been around for a very long time, it could include everything that has ever happened, and that would mean an infinite number of facts. That is why historians have to choose their facts, the ones they feel are relevant to their particular historical enquiry. Then they must arrange them into some sort of story, for bare facts are of little use without historical interpretation. Why do they matter? What do they mean? These are the questions a historian must ask, and each will come up with his or her own answers. But before they go about collecting evidence, historians must have a reason for looking, a question in mind, and that question will determine what evidence is found, and how it is interpreted. Two historians reading the same text, but asking different questions, will choose different facts, and tell quite separate stories. You need not be a historian to realise this, you need only read the newspaper.

Take any two newspapers, for newspapers are only histories of the previous day. The events that the editors have decided were important, the stories told by the journalists, are never identical. Compare these versions of the previous day to your own version of that day: how much of your experience can be found in these newspapers, or that of your friends, colleagues and family? For almost all of us, our life experience will not appear in any history, and the facts of our existence will be ignored by the generations to come. This is because those who write history do not know these facts, are not interested in them, do not deem them important. We shall be consigned to the past, but we shall not be part of history, because history is not the past, only the historian's interpretation of a very small part of it.

History, therefore, is a subjective discipline, and historians do not always agree on what evidence is important, or on what it means. And so, with each new generation of historians, previous histories are revised by those who look at different evidence, and ask different questions about it. No longer must we settle for the history of kings and queens and senior politicians, for all areas of the past are now open to enquiry, and earlier histories are open to question. This has led to different interpretations of the past, and sometimes different chronologies. There is no consensus on when the Industrial Revolution began, or when it ended, or even if it *has* ended. Historians disagree about the timing and nature of the medieval period, the early modern period, and the modern period, and I have seen extremely heated arguments over the very idea of a postmodern period. All of this begs the question, whom do you trust? The answer to that, I suspect, is nobody. History will always be a matter of opinion, but it is an opinion based on evidence. So trust nobody, demand the evidence (the so-called historical facts), and draw your own conclusions.

This, of course, is a bit much to ask, since few of us have the time to beaver away in archives, checking evidence and pondering upon it, but that is not necessary in practice. You can simply check whether you are being offered any evidence in the first place, and whether the historian is making it possible for you to check it, even if you don't actually bother to. And this is where notes come in. George Matlock, the Oxford medieval historian, wrote:

> every time you encounter evidence taken from a primary source, ensure you have the necessary information to check it for yourself. You need not check it, of course, but the knowledge that somebody might is sufficient incentive for the historian to check his or her own facts, and in itself raises the reader's confidence in the point being made, and in the validity of the evidence that supports it.

This is one of the basic rules of history, and the fact that you cannot check this quote may (given the topic being discussed) lead you to doubt its authenticity. You would, of course, be absolutely right, since the quotation and the historian are entirely made up. And that, paradoxically, makes the point valid.

Now I'm not suggesting for a moment that historians who do not use notes – who seem to be so common in popular history (and magic history) – are inventing their evidence, but there are three very good reasons why this history will be providing notes. First, it is a basic part of the job, and I want to look professional. Second, previous histories of the Indian rope trick have continually failed to check the evidence properly, and that has resulted in some blatant errors which this history seeks to correct. Third, and perhaps most importantly, many of the events and characters in this book are so bizarre that you, the reader, might wonder whether they actually happened, whether they really said what I claim they said. At that point, you may wonder whether I am being truthful and accurate, whether I can be trusted. And that would hurt my feelings. So if, at any point, you feel this way, check the Notes at the back (I am using endnotes rather than footnotes to avoid distracting you from the main narrative), and you will find the source I have used. The more cynical among you, and you know who you are, can then check that source at a reference library or, in some cases, a private archive. I realise that few, if any, of you will bother to do this but, to paraphrase the great George Matlock, the knowledge that you could if you wanted to (and that anybody else could) should make the evidence that much more convincing. Bear in mind, however, that this will not be the case for every statement; that would be unbearable. For the most part the notes will refer only to direct quotes, for these are the voices of the past and carry greater authority than any historian's prose. More general points about the past should not be controversial but, if you feel that strongly about it, they may be confirmed in other history books on the period in question. After all, historians do not disagree about everything.

And if all of this has made you wonder whether any historian can be trusted, that is no bad thing. We all have our agendas, our biases and prejudices, none of us is objective.

This history is intended, first and foremost, to be an entertaining story. No doubt some fellow historians might consider it a little simplistic in parts, might feel the humour is misplaced or misleading, might even think that it gives an unfair impression of some of the characters. Fair enough. But it is a true story nevertheless, backed up by evidence that can be checked. It is not the whole truth, any more than *The History of the World* is the whole history of the world. It is, however, and you can trust me on this (or you can check up for yourself), the most accurate and complete history of the legend of the Indian rope trick to date. And that, finally, is all it claims to be.

Dr Peter Lamont
Research Fellow
University of Edinburgh

PROLOGUE

(Kovalam beach, South India, 1997)

It is late afternoon on the beach, and this would look like paradise but for the silhouette of a fat woman in baggy shorts. She stands directly in front of a perfect setting sun, a big black figure in a floppy hat and a tangerine aura, and I wonder what she is doing here. The tourist season has not yet begun, but she may have come off-season. A discount package deal from London, perhaps, once the seat of power for those who ruled India, who boasted of an empire on which the sun never set. Now the empire has gone, the sunsets are back, and this child of empire has returned to gaze upon them for a fortnight, to savour the illusion of paradise. India is not paradise, of course, but it is a land of illusion, and it is an illusion that has brought me here too, one that became the greatest legend of the East.

According to the legend, a magician throws one end of a rope into the air. It rises into the sky until the rope is completely vertical. A boy then climbs up the rope until he gets to the top. There, in broad daylight and surrounded by the audience, the boy disappears. The legend became known as the Indian rope trick, and many came to believe it was real. Some went in search of this miracle, and there were those who claimed they had seen it for themselves. Magicians debated long and hard, large rewards were offered in the hope of attracting a performance, bizarre theories were put forward in an attempt to explain how it might be done, but nobody was able to perform it successfully. Some managed to produce a version of the trick on stage with the advantages of limited angles and overhead support. Others tried to perform it in open ground, as the legend describes, but could do little more than make a rope rise a few feet. In such conditions, nobody could make a boy vanish at the top of a rope. So when I heard that the legendary rope trick was to be performed in India, I was initially sceptical, and I still am. But I am here nonetheless, and I wonder what I shall see.

For the moment, however, there is nothing to see, not even the sunset. The rope trick will be performed on a different beach, where I hope I shall have a better view. For now, the rope trick remains a legend, but one that has been surrounded in much mystery. For the last century, its roots have been lost, and nobody quite knew how a trick that was never performed became the world's most famous illusion, how it rose above the many other miracles of the East. It was only recently that I found this out myself, so it is only now that the story can be told. It is a story about how the Victorians constructed an image of the mystic East, about those who sought to exploit this image, and those who tried to destroy it. It is a story of how a legend emerged from a world of deception and propaganda, of the extraordinary characters who helped it grow, and of how the man who started it all was forgotten.

PART I

THE RISE OF THE MYSTIC EAST

I

Extraordinary Tales from India

Hundreds of years ago, long before anybody had heard of the Indian rope trick, there were many wonderful stories to come out of India. Marco Polo told of Kashmiri conjurors who could 'bring on changes of weather and produce darkness, and do a number of things so extraordinary that no one without seeing them would believe them'.[1] And those who followed in Marco's footsteps reported many more remarkable feats. Ibn Battuta, the Moroccan traveller of seven centuries ago, was devastated by what two yogis showed him while he was a guest of the Emperor in Delhi. 'One of them assumed the form of a cube and arose from the earth,' he told his readers, 'and in this cubic shape he occupied a place in the air over our heads. I was so much astonished and terrified at this that I fainted and fell to the earth.' The delicate Moroccan was soon administered some medicine, and slowly sat up, no doubt relieved that he had imagined it all, but then saw 'this cubic figure still remaining in the air, just as it had been. [Another juggler] then took out a sandal [which] ascended, until it became opposite in situation with the cube. It then struck it upon the neck, and the cube descended to the earth.' This was all too much for the poor traveller, who once again 'took palpitation of the heart, until the Emperor ordered me medicine which restored me'. What further wonders might have been witnessed we shall never know, as the Emperor took pity on the dazed visitor, telling him, 'had I not entertained fears for the safety of thy intellect, I should have ordered them to show thee greater things than these'.[2]

Over the following centuries, many more ventured East to find what could not be found at home. Before the end of the fifteenth century, the Portuguese had sailed the long and difficult route round the Cape, and arrived in search of valuable spices. Before the sixteenth century ended – barely a few hours before it ended – the English East India Company was formed. It was not long until the Company was negotiating with the Moghul empire, and the seventeenth century saw British and French merchants competing with each other to exchange silver bullion for indigo, cotton, silk and spices. Meanwhile, Protestant and Catholic missionaries competed for the souls of the natives, though their theological assertiveness was not always welcome. Hindus and Muslims often resented the spiritual arrogance of their Christian guests, and Company merchants disliked the idea of religion getting in the way of business. Yet the missionaries continued to come, to do their God's work and to save the souls of the unfortunate, and together these adventurous plunderers of faith and fortune sowed the seeds of empire. In doing so, however, they encountered events so extraordinary that both their spiritual momentum and their business zeal were interrupted; so strange that they found time in their hectic schedules to tell those at home of what they had seen.

Some of these tales are little known today, such as the story of the great ape who could 'divine and prophesy'. This remarkable primate was owned by a Bengali juggler, and the miracle reported by Sir Thomas Roe, British Ambassador to India in the early seventeenth century. Sir Thomas had been sent by King James to the court of the Great Moghul Emperor Jahangir at Ajmere. He had hoped to win concessions for English merchants, but could not resist reporting 'an apish miracle which was acted before this King'. According to Sir Thomas, the clairvoyant ape was tested three times by Jahangir. At first, the Emperor hid his finger ring when the ape was not looking, but the ape had no trouble in divining its secret location. This aroused the curiosity of the Emperor, who decided on a more fitting test for the company, which included both Christians and Muslims. He had the names of 'twelve law-givers', including Moses, Jesus and Mohammed, written on twelve pieces of paper, and these were placed into a bag. The bag was shaken, and with the papers thus mixed, Jahangir 'bade the beast divine which was the true law'. The ape promptly reached into the bag and picked out the paper inscribed with the name of Jesus. Puzzled, but now suspicious that the ape was somehow being cued by his owner, the Emperor wrote out the names again, this time in a code known only to himself. Yet the ape was not to be defeated, and once again it chose the name of Jesus. The ape's success deeply angered a senior Muslim courtier present, who suspected this might be part of a Jesuit plot to convert the Emperor to Christianity, and who demanded one last trial, 'and offered him selfe to punishment if the ape could beguile him'. This foolhardy courtier wrote out the names of the twelve prophets, but placed only eleven papers into the bag, keeping the one with Jesus' name to himself. When the ape was offered the bag, however, he refused all the papers inside. Jahangir, unaware of the circumstances, ordered the ape to remove a slip of paper, but 'the beast tore them in fury, and made signes the true lawgivers name was not among them'. Precisely what these signs were, we are not informed, but the Emperor clearly understood them, because he demanded to know where the twelfth paper was, grabbing the courtier by the hand, and discovering the piece of paper on which was written the name of Jesus. What punishment was bestowed upon the beguiled courtier is not explained, but Jahangir decided to keep the great ape who, clairvoyant or not, was most certainly 'a good Christian'.[3]

And yet the Emperor's wonderful new pet never made it into the royal memoirs. Jahangir, a notoriously drunken and bad-tempered ruler, was not easily impressed, and only the most extraordinary miracles came to be recorded there. The Moghul emperors have all left their legacies to the world. Jahangir's father, Akbar, had united Hindus and Muslims under an image of a semi-divine king. His son, Shah Jahan, would oversee the construction of the Delhi Fort and the Taj Mahal. But the most wonderful legacy of Jahangir himself must be the accounts of the fantastic feats performed at his court by a troupe of seven Bengali jugglers. In these memoirs, the absence of the clairvoyant ape is compensated for by twenty-eight other bizarre demonstrations and a bewildering assortment of animals. Some of these we shall hear of shortly but, for the moment, the twenty-third performance is most relevant to our story. According to Jahangir, the performers:

> produced a chain of 50 cubits in length, and in my presence threw one end of it towards the sky, where it remained as if fastened to something in the air. A dog was then brought forward, and being placed at the lower end of the chain, immediately ran up, and reaching the outer end, immediately disappeared in the air. In the same manner a hog, a panther, a lion, and a tiger were successively sent up the chain and all equally disappeared at the upper end of the chain. At last they took down the chain and put it into a bag, no one ever discovering in what way the different animals were made to vanish into the air in the mysterious manner described.[4]

In the twentieth century, this story would be compared to the Indian rope trick, but Jahangir would never have made such a comparison, and neither would any of his contemporaries. They knew of no Indian rope trick, nor could they, for the legend had not yet been born. They only knew of a chain trick that was one of many reported by Jahangir, and which was by no means the one that had most impressed him.[5] And these various stories were known only to those who read Persian. Until the memoirs were translated into English in the nineteenth century, the West would have to make do with the tales of the early European visitors, and they did not know of an Indian rope trick either, though they reported many other wonders. They spoke of jugglers – for 'jugglers' was the name commonly given at this time to the wonder-workers of India – who could:

> tell any person his thoughts, cause the branch of a tree to blossom and to bear fruit within an hour, hatch an egg in their bosom in less than five minutes, producing whatever bird may be demanded, and made to fly about the room; and execute many other prodigies that need not be enumerated.[6]

And of all these early wonders, the one that attracted most attention began with a stick. Such was the case, at least, in the version reported by Jean-Baptiste Tavernier, the seventeenth-century French visitor. According to him, a group of jugglers:

having taken a small piece of stick, and planting it in the
ground, they asked one of the company what fruit he wished
to have. He replied that he desired mangoes, and then one of
the conjurers, covering himself with a sheet, stooped to the
ground . . . At each time he raised himself, the stick increased
under the eye, and at the third time it put forth branches and
buds. At the fourth time the tree was covered with leaves, and
at the fifth we saw the flowers themselves.

But before the tree could grow any further, an English
chaplain observing the jugglers:

> protested that he was unable to consent that Christians should
> be present at such spectacles, and when he saw that from a
> dry piece of wood these people in less than half an hour had
> caused a tree of four or five feet in height, with leaves and
> flowers, as in springtime, to appear, he insisted on breaking
> it, and proclaimed loudly that he would never administer the
> communion to anyone who witnessed such things in future.[7]

The righteous interruption of the chaplain curtailed this
particular performance of the 'mango trick', but there were
many others who spoke of those who 'raise a Mango-Tree, with
ripe Fruit upon its Branches, in the space of one or two Hours'.[8]
The mango trick would become one of the most famous feats
of Indian juggling. Two centuries later, it would be discussed as

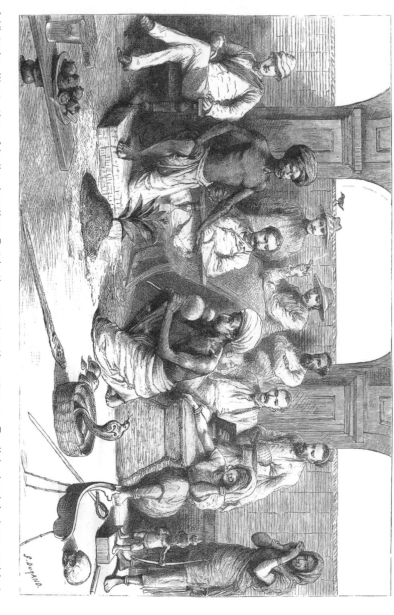

A Victorian illustration of Indian juggling. But in the seventeenth century an English chaplain 'was unable to consent that Christians should be present at such spectacles'.

an example of Indian magic brought about by hypnosis, but there was no discussion of hypnosis by these early visitors. There was, after all, no theory of hypnosis in the seventeenth century. Mesmerism did not appear until a century later (and hypnotism would not be spoken of until the century after that). There was, on the other hand, a great deal of fear about magic and witchcraft in seventeenth-century Europe, and while some of these travellers viewed these feats as deception, others spoke of black magic.

The powers of darkness were, after all, taken very seriously at home, and at the highest levels. King James I of England (VI of Scotland) had himself written a book on witchcraft, and had ordered copies of Reginald Scot's *Discoverie of Witchcraft* published in 1584 to be burned. And this, it should be pointed out, was not professional jealousy, but stemmed from the King's fear that Scot's message – that witches were harmless and magic ineffective – was a dangerous piece of propaganda. All over seventeenth-century Europe, harmless witches and ineffective magicians were abused, tortured and killed in the name of God, if not with His approval, and it is hardly surprising that European visitors to India at this time could regard an inexplicable feat with a fruit plant as something of darker significance. In one case, 'a Gentleman who had pluckt one of these Mangoes, fell sick upon it, and was never well as long as he kept it'.[9]

Yet the mango trick was not yet well known outside India. The books of these early travellers were too expensive for the vast majority of their contemporaries at home to afford, and literacy rates too low for such tales to be widely read. It was not until the nineteenth century that cheaper editions and, if necessary, English translations were printed by the growing number of publishers who supplied the expanding readership of that century.[10] It was then that these tales became truly popular, in the modern world of the Victorians, in what they proudly called the wonderful century.

By the nineteenth century, Emperor Jahangir's audience had broadened considerably. His memoirs were translated into English in 1829, and extracts were printed in the popular *Illustrated London News*, though they did not mention the chain trick at all. Instead, their large readership was faced with the Emperor's account of how jugglers had 'produced a man whom they divided limb from limb, actually severing his head from his body. They scattered these mutilated members along the ground,' then covered him with a sheet. Moments later, the man was in 'perfect health and condition, and one might have safely sworn that he had never received wound or injury'. And this was 'outdone' by the next account, which told of how two tents had been set up and shown to be empty:

Thus prepared, [the jugglers] said they would undertake to bring out of the tents any animal we chose to mention, whether bird or beast, and set them in conflict with each other. Khaun-e-Jahaun with a smile of incredulity, required them to show us a battle between two ostriches. In a few minutes, two ostriches of the largest size issued, one from either tent, and attacked each other with such fury that the blood was seen streaming from their heads . . . they continued to produce from either tent whatever animal we chose to name, and before our eyes set them to fight in the manner I have attempted to describe.[11]

Victorians reading this seventeenth-century account might well have been lost for an explanation, since few would have been aware of Jahangir's huge appetite for wine and opium, but they would not have regarded it as black magic. Jahangir's new and larger Victorian audience was living in a very different world from that of his contemporaries. It was the Victorians who witnessed the birth of the modern world, and that meant many things. The modern world was urban, more so than any previous world had been. For the first time, more people were living in towns than in the country, and more people were living than ever before. This growing urban population could wonder at the progress they had made. For the first time in human history, it was possible to travel faster than on horseback, and to communicate at huge distances without going further than the nearest telegraph office. Such technological advances had been made possible by science, and the modern world was nothing if it was not scientific.

In their wonderful world of progress, the Victorians prided themselves on being rational, no longer victims of past credulity, and were dismissive of magic and superstition. In the words of the great sociologist, Max Weber, the modern world was 'dis-enchanted' as it embraced the forces of science and technology. This process of dis-enchantment had followed from the so-called Enlightenment of the late seventeenth and eighteenth centuries. Then it was, so the story went, that men had founded an Age of Reason, when scientific knowledge and rational thinking had superseded the naive fears of the days of witchcraft. Reasonable men had considered the question of magical and miraculous phenomena, and had come to the conclusion that such events were not consistent with the evidence for how the world worked. It had, of course, never been that simple, for certain miracles were central to the Christian faith. Those who had questioned the miracles of the Bible had been regarded as quite unreasonable, and had suffered accordingly. In the late seventeenth century, Thomas Woolston, who had dismissed the Resurrection as a 'bare-faced imposture', lost his job, was fined and gaoled, and subsequently died in a debtors' prison.[12] David Hume, one of the great philosophers of the eighteenth century, had been equally dismissive of miracles, though by then he had to suffer only the occasional insult. Nevertheless, the lines of reason had been drawn, so that the Victorians could hang on to the Christian miracles while simultaneously boasting of their scepticism in relation to all other impossibilities.

Modern readers of Marco Polo's travels could therefore safely nod as the Victorian editor admonished the great traveller for 'some statements from which our belief must be withheld . . . [as he] shared that spirit of credulity which was then general over the world, and particularly through the East'.[13] Such credulity was no longer imaginable in the West, but the East continued to be associated with primitive, irrational, and superstitious thinking. Looking eastwards, the West could congratulate itself on how modern it had become. But it could also see a vital source of the raw materials that fuelled the Industrial Revolution, underpinned international trade, and greatly profited the richest economy in this ever-changing world. By the nineteenth century, the British had become the dominant European power in India and, in 1813, the East India Company monopoly had ended to allow competition among traders. As British economic and political influence grew, so too did confidence in their cultural role. Missionary activity was now seen as part of a broader civilising process that would, in turn, ease economic and political expansion. Because, of course, the modern world was imperial, ruled by the most powerful and wealthy people on earth, and the purpose of empire was to maintain this power and increase this wealth.

Greed, however, is not an attractive trait, even to the most modern of people, so other reasons were given for the exploitation of the East. One of the most popular was the need to educate their colonial subjects in modern ways, to help them see the falsity of their primitive superstitions, and to eradicate the gullibility that had plagued their own Western ancestors. Through regular complaints in the British press of native superstition and barbaric practices, the primitive state of India was demonstrated, and the need for colonial rule justified. Historians today can see this process as part of a widespread Western discourse, now referred to as Orientalism, through which the Occident constructed an image of the Orient as dark and uncivilised.[14] In India, the message was communicated in a variety of ways. The Victorian bestseller *Confessions of a Thug*, published in 1839, described how rural bandits robbed and killed not so much for material gain as to satisfy their bloodthirsty goddess Kali.[15] The extent of thuggee was often exaggerated, as was the practice of suttee, the ritual burning of a widow upon her deceased husband's funeral pyre. This was, in some parts of India, virtually non-existent, and where it did occur its causes were often a combination of social and personal tensions. In that sense, at least, it was not so different from being killed by a community for suspicion of witchcraft, and one could still find cases of that in nineteenth-century rural Britain. Yet it was portrayed by colonial officials as a typical example of primitive India, an act undertaken by widows 'of their own accord and pleasure', and one so widespread that 'all castes of

Hindoos would be extremely tenacious of its continuance'.[16] Meanwhile, missionaries railed against the practice of human sacrifice, pointing to it as an example of the barbarities of Hinduism, despite the authorities being unable to find any evidence of it having taken place.[17]

As for Indian jugglers, who would become one of the most prominent images of India, they were presented as evidence of a native tendency towards deceit on the one hand, and credulity on the other. Victorians read how these devious jugglers deceived a susceptible native population, 'illustrating the subtle ingenuity of the Hindooes, whose national character often exhibits an ability that only wants leading in the right direction to constitute them most useful members of society'.[18] Under the guidance of their colonial rulers, however, this deceitful tendency would be controlled, and Indian subjects would no longer be victims of the pretended miracles of Indian jugglers. There was, after all, no place for miracles in the modern world, other than those in the Bible. And so the Victorians dismissed all the extraordinary tales of their ancestors as the product of imposture and delusion. The primitive East, like the primitive past, would learn that the age of miracles was over. Meanwhile, for those who knew this already, no longer would tales from the East impress, for the modern West cared no more for such childishness. And it went without saying, of course, that the most powerful people on earth could not be deceived by such nonsense.

Nevertheless, there remained in this dis-enchanted modern world the potential for wonder. For even the most powerful of people need wonder, and need only encounter an inexplicable event to regain a sense of mystery. Thus, there were many who came to be convinced by the seemingly unfathomable domestic mysteries of the seance room, and we shall see later how these events played their part in the rise of the mystic East. Yet even before Modern Spiritualism emerged in the middle of the century, the modern West was being baffled by more distant mysteries, and once again finding in the East what could not be found at home. And as the rational West grew more puzzled, so the image of the East became more mysterious.

In 1832, stories began to appear in the British press of a 'man that sat in the air'. Readers of the *Saturday Magazine* must have been taken aback by the illustration of a fakir sitting cross-legged four feet from the ground. Turning to the story, they would have read of Sheshal, a Madras Brahmin who had floated in the air while engaged in prayer. If they had read the full story, they would have discovered the clue to Sheshal's secret. For the Brahmin had not been seen rising from the ground. Prior to his aerial suspension, he had been concealed from the audience by a blanket. When the blanket had been removed, Sheshal had been seen sitting in the air, his hand resting on a staff that touched the ground. The writer of the article had even pointed out that Sheshal had a metal support

Sheshal, the man that sat in the air while his secret was exposed, yet continued to bewilder the British.

connected to the staff and worn under the clothes of the performer.[19] But it seems that many did not read the full story, or if they did, they did not take it in, and Sheshal's levitation became a topic of great discussion and much mystery. 'For a while,' wrote the *Leisure Hour* two decades later, 'there was nothing heard or talked of but this wonderful "man that sat in the air". Newspapers were full of him; private letters teemed about him,' and many thought this Eastern miracle was the result of 'some wonderful discovery in magnetism'. When, in 1853, a British resident of Madras exposed the secret, the same secret that had already been disclosed in the original report, it 'made people wonder how they could ever have been so simple as not to guess at the truth long before'.[20] Now armed with the truth for a second time, the sceptical Victorians would persist in being baffled by the floating fakir. Two further decades on, the *Daily News* would surrender to this inexplicable mystery. 'Without apparatus of any kind,' the popular daily exclaimed, 'the Indian juggler walks into your garden, and suddenly appears six feet from the ground, sitting cross-legged, with nobody and nothing nearer to him than the grass. How does he do it? We cannot explain.'[21]

If this were not enough, further insoluble mysteries appeared, and some of them seemed so barbaric as to upset modern sensibilities. In 1834, the Reverend Hobart Caunter described how a juggler had placed an eight-year-old girl, 'a model for a cherub', beneath a wicker basket on the ground.

Then 'the man had seized a sword . . . and to my absolute consternation and horror, plunged it through [the basket], withdrawing it several times, and repeating the plunge with all the blind ferocity of an excited demon [until] the blood ran in streams from the basket'. In his horror, Reverend Caunter's 'first impulse was to rush upon the monster and fell him to the earth; but he was armed, and I defenceless. I looked to my companions – they appeared to be pale and paralyzed with terror.' Moments later, the basket was shown to be empty, and the girl appeared nearby in perfect health. At that point, the good Reverend calmly decided that he must have been the victim of 'a deception', but he clearly had absolutely no idea what had gone on.[22] In fact, he had just witnessed the 'basket trick', a performance of which a few years later almost caused a riot.

Prior to this performance in the yard of the barracks at Madras, the commanding officer was asked to place a guard around the performing arena. By the time the performer had repeatedly plunged the sword into the basket, and 'the cries of the girl became faint', the audience had become distinctly uncomfortable:

And well it was for the chief performer in that he had requested a guard to be placed, for it required all the exertion of this guard to prevent the aroused soldiery, who believed this to be no trick, but a piece of diabolical butchery, from leaping into the arena and tearing the man to pieces. The excitable Irishmen among the number, in particular, ground their teeth against one another, and muttered language not very complimentary to the juggler. Even the officers, whose better education and experience made them less open to such feelings, grew pale with uneasiness.[23]

Aware of the imminent threat of a stampede, the performer quickly knocked over the basket, showing it to be completely empty, the girl appeared among the crowd, ran towards the worried performer, and hugged him affectionately. The crowd fell silent, as the Irishmen stopped grinding their teeth and muttering uncomplimentary language, and 'the astonishment of the assembly was immeasurable'. Over the following years, bestselling Victorian periodicals regularly spoke of the basket trick, admitting that 'no European that witnesses it can discover [its secret]', noting how 'hundreds of shrewd hard-headed unimaginative and scientific Englishmen have seen it, thought about it, tried it – and been baffled', and wondering whether it might in fact be a supernatural phenomenon.[24]

In that same decade of floating and infanticidal fakirs, more symbolic feats were also read about. Indeed, in the very same year as the young Victoria ascended to the throne in the midst of unprecedented pomp and ceremony, a fakir descended into the Indian ground to be buried alive without food, water or air. Both survived their respective ordeals, but the latter must have caused more surprise. It was at the court of Ranjit Singh, the Sikh King of the northwest regions, that this fakir survived being buried alive for a month. Witnesses to this feat included Sir Claude Martin Wade, who provided a narrative for James Braid. Braid was the main proponent of neuro-hypnotism, later known simply as hypnotism, and he went on to find several other accounts of buried fakirs. This evidence, he stated, 'must set the point at rest for ever as to the fact of the feats referred to having been genuine phenomena'.[25] In Braid's view, these fakirs survived being buried alive through a form of self-hypnosis (though he pointed out that the Resurrection of Jesus remained a genuine miracle, on the grounds that He had received a mortal wound from a spear).[26] Hypnotism, however, was itself a mysterious phenomenon, and to offer it as an explanation was hardly to remove the sense of wonder surrounding the live burial. The popular press did not help. The *Leisure Hour* confidently pointed out that 'it appears almost incredible that some artifice was not resorted to', without providing the vaguest clue as to what sort of artifice they had in mind.[27] Meanwhile, the extremely popular *Family Herald* claimed that 'all seems and is *bona fide*', and linked the live burial to yoga and the occult.[28]

There was, to say the least, a great deal of confusion among the Victorians about how to explain all this. Some felt that these seemingly inexplicable feats suggested powers unknown in the West. Others wanted to dismiss it all as imposture and delusion, but had no idea where to begin. Many Christians, on the other hand, recognised the religious significance of these miracles. After all, it was said more than once that the 'slow progress of Christianity [in India was due to the fact] that wonders were never rare enough in the East to be generally accepted as proofs of a Divine mission, things equally surprising being performed daily'.[29] Evangelicals, keen to distinguish, as James Braid had done, between the miracles of Indian jugglers and the miracles of Jesus, published a popular book that argued for the reality of all biblical miracles and the falsity of all others, the argument for the latter being based largely on guesswork. Snake handling, a feat that some Christians today present as a genuine miracle of the Holy Spirit, was dismissed by these Victorian evangelicals as due to 'the laws which regulate the venomous secretion'.[30] Whatever that was supposed to mean, not everybody agreed that deception was involved, and the popular press argued that 'suspicions of trick in this curious process are unfounded'.[31]

Such confusion could be dangerous. During a demonstration of cobra charming in Poona, one sceptic:

> observed that he believed it was all humbug, that their teeth had been extracted, and their venom-bags cut out. At any rate, he announced his intention of collaring the first snake that came near the verandah. We objected in vain . . . with a sudden dart our friend had it by the back of the neck . . .

The old conjuror seemed terrified, and rushed at the rash Englishman, playing his pipe like a madman. But our friend kept away from him, and swung the hissing cobra in the air . . . marching all round the compound and frightening the public by pretended lunges at the faces in the crowd.[32]

In response, the crowd explained to the sceptic that his scepticism, like his sense of humour, was unique to the company, and he was finally made to realise that his demonstration, whatever it was, was not charming. He somewhat sheepishly returned the cobra to the box, 'the old charmer shut the box, sat on it, and panted. This interruption put an end to the snake-charming.' Fortunately for the sceptic, and the cobra, he was not present when another man 'stepped forward and declared he would swallow a snake'.[33]

The miraculous abilities of Indian jugglers seemed to be endless, but while some in the West came to be instilled with a deep sense of mystery, others took it all less seriously. One American reporter cheerfully recalled how 'my interpreter told me that he knew a fakir who would have a man die for me for one rupee (about 50 cents of our money). I thought this was cheap, so I invested.' Our caring reporter accompanied the fakir to his home, where the latter began to hypnotise a youth. 'After a few minutes the subject gave a leap and a yell and fell at my feet, apparently lifeless. He stood tests that would have made the average horse shout for mercy, and the fakir told me to do anything I pleased to assure myself that the man was really dead.' One can only imagine what crossed the sadistic mind of our reporter at this point, but the dead man probably got off lightly:

> I raised his eyelid and tapped his eyeball sharply with my finger, but not a muscle quivered and there was no sign that the man was anything but a corpse. As I stood there dumbfounded the fakir gave a sign, the subject jumped up with a smile, did a somersault and disappeared. It was the best 50 cents' worth I ever got.[34]

The puzzled Victorians continued to ponder on fakirs who could float in the air and live in the ground, could overcome decapitation and suffocation, could charm and devour serpents, could apparently die and come back to life. All these seemingly inexplicable feats fed the Victorian imagination, and helped create the image of the mystic East. Deprived of domestic magic, Victorians imagined an India in which anything was possible. It was from this imagined India, rather than India itself, that the legend of the rope trick would emerge. Yet the growth of the legend would depend not only on the rise of the image of the mystic East, but also on the arrival of those who sought to exploit this image and those who sought to destroy it. For there were some who saw an opportunity to profit from the mystic East, and there were others who regarded it as a threat. Both of these groups were composed, for the most part, of Western conjurors, who were less enchanted with the notion that India was the home of magic. Their response to the rise of their Indian rivals was to take what they could, and to attack what was left. And it was from this conflict that the legend would be born.

2

The Fake Fakirs

As the reputation of Indian jugglers grew, their Western counterparts saw an opportunity to exploit it. In seeking to profit from the East, however, they were doing no more than their fellow Victorians. So far as imitation is the highest form of flattery, the fake fakirs might even be regarded as radical liberals in a world of more severe forms of imperial exploitation. They did not go to India and plunder the mysteries of their Oriental colleagues. Indeed, they did not go to India at all. Instead, they sought to capitalise on a growing image of India as a land where impossibilities seemed commonplace. They did so in the interests of entertainment and, admittedly, box office receipts, in a bid to recreate the wonder of India for a public who had never been there either. And unlike many of those who did make the journey, their material gains were minimal. But most of them did it in style, some of them did it in make-up, and one of them, for reasons known only to himself, did it in French.

Colonel Stodare was an English conjuror who pretended to be French in front of English audiences. He was, therefore, a man who did not scare easily. His first recorded performance was in Edinburgh on the night of Hogmanay, 1860–1, when the city would have been celebrating the last night of the year in the only way they knew how. He was, therefore, a man without fear, and he was also a man without a commission. This Englishman was therefore not a French colonel for at least two reasons, but he was in Scotland on Hogmanay, so neither reason mattered. What did matter was that he was there to present his new show, 'Indian Magic'. He had advertised in the *Scotsman* his 'Celebrated and Original Illusions of INDIAN or EASTERN MAGIC', but he was not taking any chances. His repertoire would include standard European tricks, as well as his faithful spirit-rapping routine. The Colonel was one of many conjurors to perform such a routine, which claimed to reproduce the phenomena of spiritualist mediums on stage. It would often be accompanied by a short speech about the credulity of spiritualists, of which the sceptical audience would generally approve. In Hogmanay Edinburgh, it was important to have the audience on your side. Nevertheless, 'Indian Magic' was billed as the main attraction, and as he peered from backstage at the roomful of rowdy Scots who awaited him, even the fearless Colonel must have had a moment of doubt. A question must surely have crossed the mind of the man who dressed up as a Frenchman in order to perform Indian magic: would it not have been better to dress up as an Indian?

He had no doubt considered the idea, after the recent limited success of the Fakir of Ava in the United States. In 1854, in a bid for recognition in the West, the Fakir of Ava had billed himself as 'Chief of Staff of Conjurors to His Sublime Greatness the Nanka of Aristaphae! who will appear in his native costume, and will perform the most Astonishing Miracles of the East!'. The kingdom of Ava was a politically unstable monarchy in Burma, where two recent kings had gone insane and had had to be put under restraint.[1] But it seems unlikely that they had been deluded by the Fakir of Ava's Astonishing Miracles, since the Fakir had been born in Essex. His real name was Isaiah Harris Hughes, and he had moved to the United States in search of fame and fortune, finally reinventing himself as a fake fakir. Wearing dark make-up, and dressed in the native costume of a place he had never visited, Isaiah promised the greatest feats of the East to the pioneers of the West, but failed to deliver. Perhaps the chief conjuror to the Nanka of Aristaphae should have known better than to try to pass off standard European illusions with exotic titles. They might have expected the miracles of an Indian fakir to include the 'Hindoo Cup Trick', and might have forgiven the 'Chinese Plate Illusion', but to out-bill these with the 'Great

African Box and Sack Feat' might have led some to suspect his Avan credentials. It was not long before the Fakir gave up his native costume for formal European evening dress, and was last heard of performing in Australia.[2]

The Colonel no doubt admired, perhaps even identified with, a man pretending to be an Indian in the Wild West, but he had not followed in his tracks. Perhaps he would have if he had only realised in what prestigious company he would have been. After all, the first to don make-up and turban to perform magic was the man who created David Copperfield. Charles Dickens was, in fact, an enthusiastic amateur conjuror. As such, he took a keen interest in Indian juggling, and a somewhat cynical interest in the feats of spiritualist mediums, the journals he edited regularly taking a swipe at these 'spirit jugglers'. Dickens's writings were, of course, well known to his contemporaries, but very few people knew of his performance as 'The Unparalleled Necromancer Rhia Rhama Rhoos'. This was in part because it had taken place on the Isle of Wight. In 1849, in a charity performance for the children in the town of Bonchurch, Dickens had blacked up his face and hands, dressed himself in exotic robes, and presented himself with an Indian name, though his tricks bore very little resemblance to Indian feats. In fact, with the exception of his name and costume, there was nothing particularly Indian about the performance, an idea that would be faithfully copied by the Fakir of Ava a few years later.[3]

It was not an idea copied by the Colonel, however, who must have been relieved, while waiting backstage in Edinburgh, fearlessly wiping his sweaty brow with an imitation French handkerchief, that it was not covered in dark make-up. In fact, far from copying Dickens or the Fakir, the Colonel had decided on quite the opposite. Rather than dressing up as an Indian to perform European tricks, he had dressed up as a European to perform Indian tricks. Though he could not claim originality for this idea either. Robert-Houdin, the pioneering French conjuror, had already employed intricate mechanical methods to produce an illusion similar to the mango trick for his sophisticated Parisian audiences. He had also modified Sheshal's illusion of the 'man that sat in the air' to create 'suspension éthéréenne', in which his son was suspended in mid-air, supposedly due to the mysterious properties of ether. Unlike the Colonel, Robert-Houdin had not presented these tricks as being of Indian origin, but he had radically altered the methods involved, and the effects he obtained were very different from those of the Indian jugglers. In spite of this, Robert-Houdin, the man who inspired Houdini, would later be accused of plagiarism by the escapologist who took his surname.

But nobody was to accuse the Colonel of plagiarism. Whatever doubts he may have had about whether to appear in make-up or not, his Hogmanay Edinburgh performance in 1860–1 confirmed his decision to dress up as a Frenchman.

The boy that lay in the air. In 'suspension éthéréene', Robert-Houdin claimed his son was suspended by the mysterious properties of ether.

Not only did the Indian magic steal the show but also, rather than question his appropriation of the tricks of Indian jugglers, the press praised this European exponent of Indian magic over his 'more simple-minded Indian congeners, who practise with bare arms'.[4] To be fair to the Colonel, it was not only the presence of sleeves that distinguished his performance from that of Indian jugglers. He had significantly changed the way the tricks were done which, incidentally, had nothing to do with his sleeves. Nevertheless, he was clearly exploiting the growing fascination with Indian jugglers and, in the golden age of empire, it was understood that Europeans took what they wanted from India, and improved all that they came into contact with. A few years later, the Colonel was in London, drawing large crowds to Egyptian Hall, Piccadilly, to see the 'Indian Basket Trick' and the 'Instantaneous Growth of Flowers', based on the Indian mango trick. The London press billed his show as an opportunity to see for the first time these famous Indian tricks, without ever questioning why it was a Frenchman who was performing them or, for that matter, whether it was.

The search to acquire the secrets of the East was, in fact, a search for that most elusive of secrets, the secret of success. And in the quest for fame and fortune, many routes were explored. Whatever demand there was for Indian tricks performed by Indian jugglers was soon supplied by the Fakir of Oolu, who appeared at Egyptian Hall in turban and full

The lady that lay in the air. Victorians enjoyed the Fakir of Oolu's 'marvellous deeds', unaware that his real name was Alfred.

robes, surrounded by a decorative Oriental set. There is no Oolu mentioned in contemporary atlases of India, so we can assume that the Fakir, or to give him his real name, Alfred, had invented that part. Otherwise, Alfred had had a career of little originality. He had begun as an assistant to Professor Pepper at the London Polytechnic, a venue for popular science exhibitions. The most popular of these exhibitions had been 'Pepper's Ghost', an optical illusion that reproduced an image of a ghost on stage. After leaving the Polytechnic, Alfred had presented an 'improvement' of Pepper's Ghost, but this had come to the notice of the original patentees, and he had had to make a public apology in *The Times*. Moving to the United States, Alfred had obtained a second-hand version of Robert-Houdin's suspension éthéréene, itself a modified version of Sheshal's 'man that sat in the air', and he had decided to make this the centre of a new show featuring a new character, the Fakir of Oolu.[5] By 1873, he was being praised by *The Times* for his 'marvellous deeds', the most impressive of which had been invented by an Indian, modified by a Frenchman, and was now being performed by an Englishman dressed as an Indian.[6] What would the Colonel have thought?

This being, however, the wonderful century, where anything was possible, the wonders of Indian juggling could be performed by a fake Indian, a Frenchman or a fake Frenchman. They could even be performed, on occasion, by genuine Indian jugglers. From the beginning of that century,

Indians had been performing in Britain, the most famous being billed as 'The Four Surprising Indian Jugglers just arrived in this country from Seringapatam'.[7] What was surprising about them was their bewildering feats of dexterity. When the leader of the group, Ramo Samee, juggled four large brass balls, the essayist William Hazlitt described the feat as 'the utmost stretch of human ingenuity', and when he swallowed a sword, it was lauded as a 'wonderful exhibition'.[8] This was not only surprising and wonderful but was, for most London audiences, the first time they would have seen this genuinely dangerous feat. And once they had recovered from the experience, Ramo Samee would have a pistol loaded and shot directly at him. He not only survived but thrived, and became something of a celebrity as he toured around Britain and America. When Charles Dickens decided to blacken up on the Isle of Wight, the name he chose for one of his least-known characters was a combination of Ramo Samee and his successor, Kia Khan Khruse. Khruse performed similar feats to Ramo Samee, and had similar success, until he performed the 'gun trick' in Dublin, and was reportedly shot dead. Following that incident, Khruse's fame soared even higher than that of his mentor and, as the report was inaccurate, he was able to enjoy it to the full.[9]

It was only a matter of time, of course, before Western conjurors noticed the success of their Eastern rivals, and promptly borrowed what they could, and it was not only

Indian jugglers who were seen as fair game. Chinese jugglers soon arrived in the West and they, like their South Asian colleagues, were soon being imitated. The earliest success was Ching Ling Lauro, most likely an Englishman whose probable nationality suggests he used a pseudonym. Ching admitted his performance was an 'imitation of a Chinese juggler' which included ball juggling while 'sitting in the air upon nothing'. This was not, as it sounds, another version of Sheshal's the 'man that sat in the air'. Rather it was a balancing feat in which, though Ching did not sit upon anything, his feet were firmly planted on the ends of two poles.[10] Otherwise there seems to have been little to distinguish the Chinese jugglers, whatever their nationality, from the more numerous Indian jugglers. There was, according to one historian of magic, 'practically no difference between Indian and Chinese jugglers', and advertisements appeared for performers such as 'an Anglo-Chinese juggler *à la* Ramo Samee', while Phillipe, a well-known French performer, dressed in a large Chinese style robe to present 'Indian and Chinese experiments'.[11] Amid this confusion of Eastern and Western identities, Western conjurors were able to succeed in imitating the miracle-workers of the East, and none more tragically than Billy Robinson.

Billy had worked for many years simulating the feats of Victorian spiritualist mediums, and was looking for something new. When he came across a performer who went by the name of Ching Ling Foo, he realised he would not have to look any further. Foo, in this culturally ambiguous world of Eastern magic, was actually from China, and was also enjoying some success. Billy, who was actually from New York, came up with a suspiciously similar character, Chung Ling Soo. Soo, like Foo, performed Chinese-looking tricks in Chinese costume, and claimed to be Chinese. This upset Foo, who was not only Chinese but had thought of it first. Soo, however, refused to submit to the claims of the original Chinese magician. After a public confrontation, in which Soo 'out-Chinesed the Chinaman', Foo returned to China, while Soo went on to international success, and an expanded repertoire. Always with an eye for the dramatic, Soo decided to include the gun trick, a trick originally performed by Indian jugglers and one that was still being performed in India. In 1876, for example, *The Times* informed its readers of an unknown juggler in India 'who pretended to possess some power which rendered his life proof against any attempt that might be made upon it with powder and ball'. This courageous fellow had a man shoot at his head with a loaded gun, confident in his ability to survive the ordeal as Kia Khan Khruse had done in Dublin. The man fired the gun, shot the unknown juggler through the head, and was charged with murder, while *The Times* dryly debated the legal complications of such a scenario.[12] Some years later in London, Chung Ling Soo, the American who had begun his successful career by copying a genuine Chinese juggler, ended it by copying a genuine Indian juggler, when he was shot dead on the stage of the Wood Green Empire.

The mysteries of the East seemed to offer endless possibilities to ambitious Western conjurors, yet few of these were ever realised. Even those who avoided being shot, or having to move to Australia, never managed to provoke the sense of wonder that Indian juggling came to be associated with. Victorian audiences might enjoy their shows, but they were in no doubt that they were watching mere trickery. The rise of the modern West had, after all, been a battle against mystery and magic, a battle fought and largely won by science. Through science, all could be explained and accounted for, and there was no longer room for miracles, except for the ones in the Bible. This view was shared by the conjurors who borrowed from the East. As far as they were concerned, there had been a time when conjurors had been associated with genuine magical powers, but these days were in the past. In the modern world, conjurors now performed Modern Magic, which was scathing about any claims to supernatural abilities. Robert-Houdin founded the 'scientific school' of conjuring, which presented tricks as being entirely reliant upon scientific laws. Colonel Stodare was absolutely clear that his tricks were perfectly in accordance with the known laws of nature.[13] Both of them publicly denounced the supernatural claims of spiritualist mediums, and Billy Robinson even published a book on the subject.[14]

Yet even the most modern of people needed wonder, and since genuine wonders were being dismissed at home, many began to look elsewhere, to a mysterious East that seemed to offer other possibilities. Images of this mysterious East were also available in popular literature, such as Wilkie Collins's bestseller, *The Moonstone*, published in 1868. Collins was a friend of Dickens, and just as popular among the Victorians. *The Moonstone* has the peculiar claim to be the first detective mystery novel in the English language, the mystery surrounding a missing Indian diamond, and a sense of mystery surrounding a troupe of Indian jugglers. The only feat of juggling described is a demonstration of clairvoyance performed by a small boy accompanying the jugglers. The boy pours ink into his palm and, in a form of scrying more popularly associated with a crystal ball, sees into the future. Collins almost certainly got this idea from a well-known account of alleged clairvoyance from Egypt.[15] Yet, at a time when many confused different parts of the East, it was interpreted as 'a development of the romantic side of the Indian character'.[16]

It would have been more accurate, however, to say that this was a development of the romantic side of the British character. For the British, the East in general, and India in particular, was becoming a place of romance and mystery, providing the magic that was lacking in the West.[17] It was this rising image of the mystic East that Western conjurors intended to tap into when they attempted to recreate the wonder of the East. Their overt scepticism, however, prevented them from successfully exploiting the image, for it was an image based on the idea that magic was not merely unexplained but inexplicable, that magic might be real. In the modern West, this idea could be entertained only in relation to an imagined India, a far-off place where different rules might apply. It was not Indian jugglers who were surrounded in mystery so much as India itself. This was the real secret of Indian juggling, and this is precisely what Western conjurors were unable to recreate, even with dark make-up.

There were, however, other conjurors in the West who did claim to be real, and did so by employing the methods of Indian jugglers. They claimed to be able to conjure spirits by performing an Indian rope trick of their own. Indian juggling would increasingly come to be linked to the supernatural, and many would begin to regard India as the home of magic. This would anger Western conjurors in general, and one in particular. So, as some had attempted to profit from the mysterious image of India, others would set out to destroy it, and one man would become the arch-enemy of the mystic East.

3

Enemy of the Mystic East

It was not so long ago that when an Englishman went to the toilet, he thought of John Nevil Maskelyne, though if asked, he would probably have denied this. Never having been fond of urinating, the English have long preferred to 'water the flowers', 'shake a leg', or 'spend a penny'. This latter activity, which was very popular for the best part of a century, continues to be performed by the elderly, though perhaps not as regularly as it used to be. Nevertheless, they can remember when the whole of England used to spend a penny, when proud Englishmen would stand in line patiently holding their pennies, when hundreds of pounds could be spent in a single day in London. They can remember when public toilets had locks on the cubicle doors, locks that could be opened only by placing a penny into a slot. The locks that one had to negotiate if one wanted to spend a penny were made of brass, they were made to last, and they were made by John Nevil Maskelyne. His was the name a man would see just before the heavy wooden door closed behind him, and he was confronted with Armitage Shanks.

The man who patented the pay toilet was, however, a man of many talents. In those difficult days before it was possible to spend a penny, Maskelyne's name could be seen outside theatres, offering the English an alternative form of relief. He was probably the best-known conjuror of his day, a creative illusionist, a talented juggler, and a pioneer of English conjuring. With his first partner, he established Egyptian Hall from 1873, Piccadilly, as the home of English magic, and with his second partner ran St George's Hall as its successor. In doing so, he provided a popular venue for many of his fellow performers, but not all conjurors were welcome there. Those who claimed to conjure spirits were, in his view, enemies to be exposed. It was, in fact, as a debunker of spiritualism that his career had begun in 1865.

Spiritualism had by then become big business. It had arisen in the middle of the nineteenth century, when orthodox Christianity was struggling against new challenges to the revealed truth of the Bible. Recent advances in geology showed that the world was much older than 4004 BC, the date suggested by the genealogy of the Old Testament. Theologians in Germany were claiming the Bible was not reliable as history. And Darwin's theory of natural selection was about to offer an alternative to the Genesis version of the origin of

John Nevil Maskelyne and his toilet toll.

species. So, at a time when science was increasingly challenging religion, what Modern Spiritualism claimed it could offer was scientific evidence of religious truth. Spiritualists believed that the phenomena occurring at seances were direct proof of the reality of miracles, and of the very existence of an afterlife.

Yet the phenomena that seemed to answer the most profound of questions were hardly of a profound nature. At first, the spirits communicated through rapping noises, though these usually required the services of a gifted medium. Those who could not attract spirit raps could resort to table-turning and table-tipping. A group would sit round a small table in their drawing room, fingers placed on the top of the table, and solemnly ask the spirits questions. If the spirits responded, the table would tip or turn, perhaps once for yes and twice for no. As Victorian engineers were struggling to perfect an electric telegraph that could send earthly messages in Morse code, the spiritual telegraph also developed more complex codes. Letter cards came to be used in conjunction with spirit-rapping, and as sitters passed their fingers over the cards, raps would sound to indicate the appropriate letter. With sufficient patience, sentences could be constructed, and the living could learn about life in the hereafter. One spirit wrote to her curious family, 'I hover around you like an angel, trying to make you happy,' while others wondered why, if spirits really could communicate with the living, they did not provide more enlightening information.[1]

Some individuals seemed to be more proficient than others at attracting spirit phenomena, and rose to fame on the back of quite bizarre demonstrations of otherworldly communication. Take, for example, the Davenport brothers, who travelled around America and Britain performing their spirit manifestations. In a typical Davenport seance, the two brothers, William and Ira, would sit on chairs inside a large wardrobe, known as a spirit cabinet. Inside this cabinet were various objects, including musical instruments. Someone from the audience would then be asked to tie the mediums tightly to the chairs with rope and, once the brothers were felt to be securely bound, the doors of the cabinet would be closed. A moment or two later, objects would fly into the air, and the instruments would be heard playing. Then it would go quiet, and someone would be asked to open the doors of the cabinet. There would be the brothers, still sitting in their respective chairs, still securely bound by rope. In such a position, they clearly could not have been responsible for the strange events that had been witnessed, and the only reasonable conclusion for many was that they had witnessed genuine spirit manifestations. Of course, not everyone was convinced, and some sceptics suggested that the brothers were somehow able to escape from the rope. But how?

It so happens that several years earlier some Indian jugglers had visited Britain and America, and among the many dexterous feats they had performed had been a rope trick. In this less than legendary feat, one of the jugglers would be tied up with rope, and then he would escape. Unlike the Davenport brothers, the juggler had not claimed any supernatural powers were involved, and sceptical contemporaries were quick to accuse the brothers of performing a modified version of this Indian rope trick. John Nevil Maskelyne started his conjuring career in 1865, when he saw the Davenport brothers perform their spirit cabinet on stage, and quickly realised how it was done. He immediately announced his intention of duplicating their so-called spirit phenomena, and before long was on stage with his own spirit cabinet, producing his own manifestations without spiritual assistance. But the brothers persisted in performing their act in theatres around Britain, despite these exposures and the occasional riot. Sometimes, the brothers were tied so tightly that the spirits were prevented from producing any phenomena at all, and the boys had to be cut free. The audience might react by storming the stage, and destroying the spirit cabinet.[2] Years later, the ability to escape from ropes, chains and other restraints would become known as escapology, and the man who made it famous, Harry Houdini, would be as well known for his public exposures of fraudulent spirit mediums. In 1907, an elderly Ira Davenport would be visited by Houdini, and the legendary escapologist would hear the confession of the medium.[3]

But back in the middle of the nineteenth century, there were those who believed that these spirit manifestations were truly supernatural. Spiritualists rejected the notion that the Davenport brothers employed the simple methods of Indian jugglers. They cited the renowned traveller, Captain Richard Burton, who had 'spent a great part of my life in Oriental lands, and have seen there many magicians', yet after four seances with the Davenports, the phenomena remained inexplicable to him.[4] Indians, on the other hand, were less impressed. According to a British resident who saw a performance of the rope escape in India, 'I told [the juggler] there were men in England who were bound in the same way, but had spirits to untie them, at which he laughed the laugh of the incredulous.'[5] One can only imagine what the laugh of the incredulous sounds like, from a man whose colonial rulers appear to be more gullible than the 'primitive natives' they rule. Curiously enough, spiritualists did think that the rope-tying feat (as performed by Indian jugglers) was trickery, but they held the view that 'these Orientals are mediums as well as conjurors'.[6] When a British financier in India, enigmatically referred to as 'Mr A', was reported to have duplicated the Davenport phenomena, spiritualists concluded that 'Mr A is possessed of the occult powers of India', and cited other 'marvellous and incomprehensible' Indian phenomena, such as the basket trick.[7] A link between Victorian spiritualism and Indian juggling was emerging, and soon it was strengthened by the exploits of the most famous medium of the century.

D. D. Home was to become the most successful medium of the century. Born in Scotland and raised in America, he conducted seances for British aristocracy and continental royalty. His sitters included writers and intellectuals such as William Makepeace Thackeray, Robert Owen and John Ruskin, prominent politicians such as the former Chancellor, Lord Brougham, and the Corn Law reformer, John Bright, and an impressive list of respectable gentlemen, lawyers, bankers and scientists. He bewildered Sir David Brewster, inventor of the kaleidoscope and later Principal of Edinburgh University. Francis Galton was so impressed that he wrote to his cousin, Charles Darwin, who himself requested a sitting with the medium. Alas, the meeting did not take place, though Darwin's co-originator of the theory of natural selection, Alfred Russell Wallace, was convinced of Home's ability to contact the spirit world. Home became something of an international celebrity: a confidante of Napoleon III, he married a god-daughter of the Czar of Russia, his best man being the author Alexandre Dumas. A sensitive, enigmatic and controversial figure, Home provoked mixed feelings among those who witnessed what he did. The poets, Robert and Elizabeth Barrett Browning, attended a seance in 1855: Elizabeth was immediately convinced she had witnessed genuine spirits, while Robert dismissed Home as a 'dungball', and later threatened to throw him down a flight of stairs.[8] But Browning, hard as he tried, was unable to explain how Home produced his extraordinary range of manifestations, and neither was anybody else, including Maskelyne.[9]

Witnesses who attended a Home seance reported all manner of wonders. Large tables would rock back and forward and rise into the air, spirit hands would materialise out of thin air and sometimes shake hands with those present, and occasionally the medium himself would levitate up to the ceiling. Home was scrutinised by sceptics and tested by scientists, but nobody could provide an adequate explanation for what they saw. Now and again, he would come up with a new miracle, and when Home began to handle red-hot coals without being burned, spiritualists made comparisons with Oriental miracles, and the spiritualist press started reporting various examples of 'fire ordeals', such as walking on hot irons and placing a red-hot iron on the tongue. There was, in fact, nothing new or particularly Eastern about 'fire ordeals'; these had been reported in ancient Britain, in the Old Testament, and occurred in many non-Western societies. The Victorians could see such feats for themselves – throughout the nineteenth century, there were performers, sometimes referred to as 'human salamanders' or 'fire-kings', who demonstrated various types of resistance to fire, such as walking into a large oven with a piece of raw meat and emerging later unscathed, holding a well-cooked steak. But this was strictly for entertainment purposes. Similar phenomena occurring in the

East, on the other hand, were regarded as having spiritual significance, and the spiritualist press described such things as 'phenomena of the Eastern nations', arguing that when Home resisted red-hot coals, he was employing supernatural abilities that had been known about in the East for thousands of years.[10] And it was not only spiritualists who were making these comparisons.

In 1869, Home floated out of the window of his London residence, then floated back in via the window of the adjacent room. That, at least, is what was reported by Viscount Adare, who bravely published his *Experiences with D. D. Home* that year, then quickly regretted what he had done and withdrew the book from circulation. It was too late, however, to prevent the newspapers from getting hold of the story. The event has since become one of the most famous feats in the history of psychical research. Some have claimed that Adare and his friends were hypnotised, some have thought Home simply jumped between the window ledges when nobody was looking. Others have seen the levitation as an example of psychokinesis – a twentieth-century term sometimes translated as 'mind over matter' – while others still have agreed with Home that this was the result of direct intervention in the mundane world by the spirits of the dead. The response of the Victorian press, however, was to compare Home to an Indian juggler. The *Observer* confidently claimed that 'an Indian juggler could sit down in the middle of

Trafalgar Square, and then slowly and steadily rise in the air to a height of five or six feet, still sitting, and as slowly come down again . . . none of Mr Home's "levitations", come anywhere near [such] simple performances'. In fact, such performances would have been far from simple, and the Indian levitation they referred to was none other than 'the man that sat in the air', a somewhat less impressive feat. But the *Observer* was one of several sceptical newspapers that wanted to debunk spiritualist phenomena as trickery, and felt that the best way to do this was to present Indian juggling as a superior form of deception. As far as the *Examiner* was concerned, 'the very poorest Hindoo juggler can beat the Spiritualists at their own tricks'.[11]

Such an approach was risky, however, and was bound to backfire. If Indian juggling was superior to what Home was doing, and if nobody actually knew what Home was doing, Indian juggling must have been that much more mysterious. Soon, the very same people who had been using Indian juggling to debunk the spiritualists would have to begin debunking Indian juggling itself, and this would prove to be a more difficult task. After all, the reputation of Indian jugglers had been growing throughout the nineteenth century. Bewildered by tales emerging from the East, the Western press had praised their seemingly inexplicable wonders, and this growing reputation had been exploited by several Western conjurors, who had dressed up accordingly in an attempt to profit from the increasingly mysterious image of the Orient. All this was harmless, as far as the majority of Western conjurors were concerned, but it was not long before things began to get out of hand. The tales from the East were normally more impressive than the feats of Indian juggling being seen on stage. Colonel Stodare might be seen to perform similar deeds, might even be praised by some for his superior presentations, but many others believed there was more to Indian juggling than was to be seen at a Stodare show. At the same time as the Colonel was performing his version of the basket trick on a British stage, sections of the British press could write of the basket trick performed by jugglers in India that 'no European can discover its secret'. Achieved without the aid of a stage by humble itinerant jugglers, some of these performances came to be seen as more mysterious than the tricks of Western conjurors. Many Victorian newspapers and journals began to speak of 'the jugglers of India, whose performances so far outstrip any of their European counterparts', who 'seem to be more expert there than here', whose feats were 'the result of surprising art [at which] the natives of India far excel the whole world'.[12]

This, of course, did not go down at all well with Western conjurors, who naturally regarded themselves as superior to their Indian rivals. It was one thing to present Indian juggling as better than the dishonest deceptions of spirit mediums, but to claim it was superior to the honest art of British conjuring was, in the minds of honest British conjurors, going too far. Yet there was a more dangerous conclusion that could be drawn from all this. Perhaps the apparent superiority of Indian jugglers could be explained another way: perhaps they were not superior conjurors after all, perhaps they had 'discovered natural laws of which we in the West are ignorant'.[13] After all, the Victorian press had claimed that Indian jugglers could better the feats of D. D. Home, yet nobody had explained how, if they were tricks, he had done them. This, of course, contributed to the rise of the image of the mystic East, but it was not an image shared by all, and it was anathema to sceptical Western conjurors. They were, in their own minds, on the front line of the war against magic and mystery that characterised the emergence of the modern world. Possessing the ability to simulate magical powers, they were always adamant they had none, and dismissive of anyone who claimed such powers. Since the appearance of spirit mediums, they had sought to expose and debunk these frauds, and for a while, Indian juggling had been on their side in the good fight. But now too many were beginning to believe that Indian juggling itself was a supernatural phenomenon. It was therefore in the interests of Western science and progress that such superstitious nonsense be nipped in the bud. Of course, their professional pride might be offended by the claim that they were inferior to Indian jugglers, but that was hardly the point. What they would do would be for the good of the Western world, and if their personal interests happened to be served in the process, that was never their intention. And so, in 1878, John Nevil Maskelyne decided to do what no conjuror is ever supposed to do – he decided to expose his Indian colleagues by explaining to the public how their tricks were done.

When Maskelyne made the decision to expose these secrets, he felt it necessary to explain himself. He began by describing the East as the home of magic, 'not the innocent conjuring we give that name to in England . . . but the crafty and sometimes audacious imposture in which the magician pretends to possess supernatural powers'. He went on to complain that 'those oily mendicants, the fakirs, whose odour of sanctity is not by any means of the sweetest, have deluded innocent Englishmen into writing of their jugglery as though it had an element of the miraculous in it'. These innocent Englishmen, 'these easy-going people', had been victims of 'the romance clinging to all things Oriental'. In such circumstances, where a romantic image of India had been so cruelly inflicted upon these innocent easy-going colonisers, retaliation was clearly justified. It was noted in passing that these cruel jugglers were not at all remarkable, unless 'remarkable for their poverty', and that 'even they recognize the superiority of the Western magician', but that was hardly the point. The point was that they, like the spirit mediums who pretended to supernatural powers, were enemies of progress and modernity. It was, therefore, in the interests of the modern world, and the innocent easy-going people who ruled it, that John Nevil Maskelyne publicly expose the tricks of poverty-stricken jugglers.

He began with the 'man that sat in the air' (the secret of which had already been revealed more than once), and went on to reveal the method of the basket trick (the secret of which he got wrong). He then discussed sword swallowing (a 'very disgusting feat' that could be 'managed without trickery by some performers with leather throats and an abnormal appetite for steel'), and ended with a condemnation of the cruelty involved in making a bird bow and speak to the audience, where the juggler 'pinches the poor thing's legs until it bends in pain and squeaks'. In a second article, Maskelyne revealed the secrets of the mango trick and snake charming, went on to denigrate Arabs, and managed to include certain secrets of a well-known French conjuror.[14] With the modern world now safe from oily mendicants and the French, Maskelyne presumably rested for a while, prior to addressing the problem of public toilet access.

Before long, Maskelyne's noble cause was taken up by several other Western conjurors whose professional pride had nothing to do with their actions. It was, wrote a renowned author of conjuring texts, 'in the interests of truth and commonsense' that Western conjurors had visited the East, and 'the alleged miracles . . . found to be perfectly easy of explanation'.[15] Over the following years, in the interests of truth and commonsense, popular periodicals were filled with articles such as 'Indian conjuring explained', 'Secrets of Indian jugglery', and 'Methods of Hindu jugglery and magic'.[16] That all of these managed to stress the superiority of Western conjurors over Indian jugglers was hardly the point. Truth and commonsense were at stake, and 'more nonsense has been written about East India fakirs and jugglers than any other class of conjurers'.[17] It had been 'almost an article of faith that the conjurors of Hindustan surpassed all others', but the 'skill of Indian jugglers [had been] greatly exaggerated'. So much so, that on witnessing the feats of the great English conjuror, Charles Bertram, Indian jugglers 'were so overcome at his performances, that they frequently fell down on the ground before him and kissed his feet in token alike of admiration and acknowledgement of his superiority'.[18]

Such adoration might not have been expressed had they known that the man whose feet they were kissing was about to publicly reveal the secrets of their livelihood. Bertram not only publicly exposed the secrets of the basket trick and the mango trick, but did so with greater accuracy than Maskelyne, and included drawings for the sake of clarity. Under attack from detailed explanations and illustrations, the reputation of Indian juggling was bound to suffer. Yet it would be able to rely on two powerful allies. The first was a large section of the British public, whose cynicism was capable of doubting even truth and commonsense, yet whose hunger for

"HE DRIVES A SWORD THROUGH THE BASKET FROM TOP TO BOTTOM."

"HE JUMPS INTO THE BASKET."

The basket trick, of which it was said 'no European can discover its secret', was exposed by Western conjurors for entirely selfless reasons.

wonder could limit even their cynicism. These most sceptical of believers refused to submit to the authority of the experts, maintained that Indian jugglers were superior to their European critics, and in the face of detailed explanations of how they were done, persisted in finding their tricks incomprehensible.[19] Such stubbornness might well have proved sufficient to save Indian jugglers' reputation, but they were soon to be joined by another more powerful Western ally. As Western conjurors were defending the innocent easy-going British empire against cruel oily mendicants whose tricks they had never wanted anyway, a new defender of the mystic East appeared. She became Maskelyne's greatest enemy, she provided inspiration for our legend, and she was unquestionably one of the most extraordinary figures of the wonderful century.

Helena Petrova Blavatsky, known to most as Madame Blavatsky, known to her followers as HPB, was also known as a medium and a magician, a guru and a charlatan. Her past, however, is largely unknown. She claimed that, during her childhood in Russia, she had been in psychic contact with stuffed animals. She also admitted a fondness for fairy tales, and told how she had run away from a marriage to a cruel elderly Russian general. She was, according to one devotee, 'of average height, sharing the family plumpness which turned to corpulence as she grew older, and had a massive face'. In the words of one spirit entity on whose behalf she regularly spoke, she was 'a woman of most exceptional and wonderful endowments'.[20] Multilingual, widely travelled, though probably not as widely as she claimed, this big bold woman in a world of men found her vocation with the arrival of Modern Spiritualism, when she began to communicate with the dead, and continued on a path of miracles that would soon lead to India.

Madame Blavatsky's introduction to the spirit world was as a result of meeting the famous medium D. D. Home. Her meeting with him was hardly congenial, however. 'I took no interest in her,' Home recalled, 'excepting a singular impression I had the first time I saw a young gentleman who has ever since been a brother to me. He did not follow my advice. He was at the time her lover, and it was most repulsive to me that in order to attract attention she pretended to be a medium.'[21] Madame Blavatsky was by no means the first large woman to pretend to be a medium. When Mrs Guppy, an equally well-endowed psychic, was said to have transported herself across London into a seance room, one unkind Victorian journalist had suggested that her arrival in the room had been assisted by ageing floorboards in the room above. Neither was Madame Blavatsky the first medium to exploit the sexual tension of the seance. There, in the middle of the Victorian world of respectability and propriety, men and women were gathering together in rooms, holding hands, and

Madame Blavatsky described herself as 'a woman of most exceptional
and wonderful endowments'.

turning the lights out. It was bound to attract an audience. Some female mediums flaunted the intimacy of the seance room to the delight of gentlemen sitters, and under spirit influence might occasionally writhe and moan in quasi-orgasmic fashion. It is quite possible that many gentlemen attending a seance sought contact with the living rather than the dead.[22]

But if Madame Blavatsky was not original in these respects, she nevertheless had a unique career. Undeterred by Home's lack of interest, she entered the medium profession, and her career could not have been less like that of Home. While the conjuror of kings was never caught cheating, Madame Blavatsky was soon in trouble. Trying to materialise a spirit hand, she was reportedly caught with a stuffed glove. This was in Egypt, and her lack of success prompted her to move to the United States. Here, she worked briefly with the Holmeses, a couple who claimed to produce full-form spirit materialisations, and who had convinced Robert Dale Owen, former US Congressman and foreign ambassador, that such manifestations were genuine. Unfortunately for the Holmeses, their stooge confessed to dressing up as the spirit, Dale Owen publicly admitted to having been duped by the mediums, and the shock of this unpleasant revelation led to his subsequent insanity. Moving to New York, Madame Blavatsky made attempts to establish a 'Miracle Club', where all manner of wonders would be demonstrated in impossible conditions, but she was unable to get the thing off the ground. It was then, in 1875, that she founded the Theosophical Society, a decision that finally resulted in success, and one that would inadvertently inspire a tale about an Indian rope trick.

The Theosophical Society was a religious organisation based on the teachings of theosophy, a collection of ideas and extracts from Hinduism, Buddhism and ancient Western philosophy, and presented by Blavatsky in what seems like no particular order. Scholars of religion dismissed her writings as 'a re-hash of Neo-Platonic and Cabalistic mysticism with Buddhist terminology', while Max Muller, the pioneer of comparative religion, described her notion of Buddhism as 'misunderstood, distorted, caricatured'.[23] If you can make it through the five substantial volumes of her two enormous works, *Isis Unveiled* and *The Secret Doctrine*, published in 1877 and 1888 respectively, it is likely that Isis will continue to be shrouded in a veil, and the doctrine will remain a secret. Mystical writings are rarely clear, which is how they remain esoteric. But presumably enough people must have understood, because the society attracted members. Unless, of course, they were there for the miracles. From the beginning, Madame Blavatsky stressed the importance of producing miraculous phenomena as 'vital proof' of the doctrines. One prominent member actually admitted that all those joining the society when he was there 'did so in the hope of mastering the secrets of magic'.[24] Theosophical writings were full of examples of magical phenomena, reports of clairvoyance and materialisations were common, and India was regularly presented as the most magical of lands.

Miraculous phenomena were available closer to home, of course, but many spiritualists were increasingly frustrated by the sceptical attitude of their fellow Westerners. One prominent spiritualist complained that 'it is not in these western countries that we must seek for [spiritual answers]. The eastern lands have been and are the fields of these studies – studies which we, in England, have resuscitated only of late, amid angry persecution and supercilious contempt from Orthodox Science and Religion.'[25] Even some who found it difficult to accept the domestic miracles of the spiritualists found it more plausible that the mysterious East might be the home of mysterious phenomena. John Nevil Maskelyne had complained of Indian jugglers who 'deluded innocent Englishmen into writing of their jugglery as though it had an element of the miraculous in it', dismissing Indian marvels as products of exaggeration 'tinged by the romance clinging to all things Oriental'. But this is just what theosophy offered: the notion of India as the home of magic. The society headquarters moved to Madras shortly after its foundation, and Madame Blavatsky described all manner of phenomena associated with India. She pointed out that hundreds of travellers had reported levitating fakirs, and complained that all of them had been dismissed as either liars or victims of hallucination. Dismissing trickery as an explanation for such phenomena, she argued that there was not 'either in India or in Ceylon, a single European, even among the oldest residents, who has been able to indicate the means employed by those devotees for the production of these phenomena'.[26] In her view, the phenomena were psychic, a then recently coined term to refer to natural but little understood forces, and one that would be replaced in the twentieth century by the term 'paranormal'. But whatever these little-understood forces were called, it was Madame Blavatsky's opinion that they were better understood in India than in the West. When an Indian correspondent questioned the importance of the phenomena to theosophical teachings, she replied that they served to demonstrate to the West the existence of powers already known in India.[27]

If India was the home of psychic phenomena, however, this made proper investigation more difficult. When the Society for Psychical Research was founded in London in 1882, to investigate scientifically alleged psychic and spiritualist phenomena, they were eager to investigate the claims of Madame Blavatsky. And if the miracles were occurring in India, then that is where they would have to be tested. So, in 1884, the SPR sent Richard Hodgson, a Cambridge graduate, to Madras to assess the reported phenomena. By the time Hodgson arrived, there had been accusations of fraud in an

Indian newspaper surrounding the so-called Mahatma letters. These were the psychic communications Madame Blavatsky claimed to receive from her Tibetan spiritual masters, the Mahatmas, who contacted her directly from Tibet either through clairvoyance or through written messages that materialised in a shrine at the society headquarters. The allegation in the newspaper, made by two former colleagues of Madame Blavatsky, was that she had written these messages herself. She, of course, denied the charge. Hodgson, after several months of investigation and the opinion of handwriting experts, decided that Madame Blavatsky was indeed the author of the letters, and that none of the reported phenomena should be taken seriously. In the light of Hodgson's report, the SPR committee concluded that there was a:

> very strong general presumption that all the marvellous narratives put forward as evidence of the existence and occult power of the Mahatmas are to be explained as due either (a) to deliberate deception carried out by or at the instigation of Madame Blavatsky, or (b) to spontaneous illusion, or hallucination, or unconscious misrepresentation or invention on the part of the witnesses.[28]

Their final judgement of Madame Blavatsky, which would appear for several decades in the *Encyclopaedia Britannica*, was that 'we regard her neither as the mouthpiece of seers, nor as a mere vulgar adventuress; we think she has achieved a title to permanent remembrance as one of the most accomplished, ingenious, and interesting impostors in history'.[29]

Such a devastating conclusion was, of course, music to the ears of John Nevil Maskelyne. In the wake of the SPR report, he remarked that 'the occult portion of Theosophy has seen its best days, and will soon be on the wane . . . If these supposed marvels are no longer flaunted in the eyes of a credulous world, the matter concerns me no more.'[30] Yet Maskelyne would later change his mind, and would publish *The Fraud of Modern Theosophy Exposed: A Brief History of the Greatest Imposture ever Perpetrated under the Cloak of Religion*. This occasionally vicious book would be not only a tirade against Madame Blavatsky and the survival of the Theosophical Society, but also an attempt to come to terms with the Indian miracle that had by then become internationally famous. A section of the book would be devoted to this supposedly miraculous feat, and the illustration on the front cover would be of that same feat: a rope rising into the air, and a boy climbing up the rope.

For it was in these intervening years that the Indian rope trick rose to fame, and with the rise of our legend, the image of the mystic East would be safe. Just a few years later, in 1899, the *Strand Magazine* would declare: 'Ask the average man for what India is most celebrated, and chances are ten to one that he will ignore the glories of the Taj Mahal, the beneficence of British rule, even Mr Kipling, and will unhesitatingly reply in one word, "Jugglers".'[31]

And when the *Strand Magazine* spoke of Indian juggling in 1899, it spoke of the most famous wonder of all: the Indian rope trick. Of all the tales of the mystic East, it would be the most extraordinary, and there would be many who told the tale. There would be a fake fakir who would seek to exploit it, and the man who succeeded John Nevil Maskelyne would do all he could to destroy it. Yet already, as the wonderful century drew to a close, the rope trick was being seen as the most famous feat of the most celebrated representatives of the greatest possession of the largest empire in the world. And this in itself was no mean achievement. For what the most powerful people on earth did not realise was that the rope trick's rise to fame had begun just a few years earlier – in Chicago.

PART II

THE BIRTH OF A LEGEND

4

Once Upon a Time in the West

John Elbert Wilkie, the man who gave birth to our legend, was born in a quite different world of secrets and deception. His life and career would rarely stray far from plots and propaganda, forgery and fraud, but throughout that career he would rely on his abilities as a story-teller to succeed. He would tell many stories, and become well known as the most public informant in the most secretive of jobs. Yet he would never be as well known as his most famous story, one that he would receive very little credit for. In 1860, however, he did not know any of this.

Wilkie was born in Chicago that year, just as his future boss was engineering the election of the next American president. Joseph Medill, managing editor of the *Chicago Tribune*, was an influential man, and one who would express strong views on a range of topics. During the Chicago labour wars, he would be for 'stringing up the leaders', while his recipe for dealing with the unemployed, whom he equated with strikers, would be 'to put arsenic in [their] food'.[1] In 1860, however, his views were less radical. He was, for some time, a supporter of William H. Seward, then favourite to be nominated as Republican candidate for the forthcoming presidential elections. Seward, a man described as 'a sloughing, slender figure with a head like a wise macaw, a beaked nose, shaggy eyebrows, red hair, a free talker, [and] a perpetual smoker', was optimistic of success with such an influential editor behind him.[2] But Medill changed his mind and he, and his *Tribune*, decided to back Seward's then lesser known opponent, a man called Abraham Lincoln. This infuriated Seward, who told Medill privately: 'You have stunned me. You advocate Lincoln in preference to me . . . I consider this a personal insult. I had always counted on you as one of my boys. Henceforth you and I are parted . . . I defy you to do your worst.'[3]

And that was precisely what Medill did. At the Republican party convention that year, Medill was in charge of seating arrangements, a task not often associated with the shaping of democracy. Medill, however, was aware of the various state allegiances, and that the most important doubtful state was Pennsylvania. He therefore positioned the undecided Pennsylvanian delegates well away from the influence of Seward supporters, and separated by Lincoln supporters from Illinois, Indiana and New Jersey, 'so far away that the voices of the Seward orators could scarcely be heard'. Lincoln, of course, won the nomination, and Medill later called this 'the meanest trick I ever did in my life'.[4] A few months later, Abraham Lincoln was President, William H. Seward was Secretary of State, and the country was engaged in civil war.

John E. Wilkie would have known nothing of the role the *Tribune* editor played in Lincoln's election, but the Civil War would have its effect on the infant. During the war, his father Franc worked as a correspondent for the *New York Times*, and quickly established himself as one of the leading war correspondents, his reports being used by several newspapers, including the *Chicago Tribune*, where young Wilkie would later work. Yet his career would not be confined to journalism and, by the end of the war, a somewhat less predictable influence on Wilkie's future had emerged. In the last cabinet meeting of the war, Lincoln established the US Secret Service, initially for spy work, but before long their primary role was to investigate the growing problem of counterfeiting after the Civil War. In years to come, their role would change to protecting the President, and John E. Wilkie would play a part in this, but in 1865 the protection of the President proved tragically impossible. President Lincoln was assassinated in Ford's Theatre while, that very same evening, Secretary Seward was attacked at home with a bowie knife, and barely escaped with his life.[5]

As a teenager, Wilkie attended Chicago High School, and while he was there, the city was devastated by the great fire of 1871. Joseph Medill's *Tribune* called on Chicago citizens to rebuild the city, a popular cry that resulted in Medill being elected Mayor of Chicago. Medill's strong anti-vice policies were resented by Chicago gangsters, however, who responded by forming a syndicate that put up a rival candidate to defeat Medill in the next election, a move that has been seen as the origins of organised crime in Chicago.[6] Wilkie was no doubt aware of all this, even as a schoolboy. Given his father's reputation as a journalist, he may have already been considering following in his footsteps. He most likely read Medill's *Tribune*, though he may not have known he would be working for him a few years later. He possibly also knew that former Secretary of State, William H. Seward, had decided to become 'the first famous American politician to make what might be called a public voyage around the world'. For as Medill was being elected Mayor of Chicago, his old enemy was enjoying being 'treated with royal distinction' in the major cities of the Orient. In India, he was 'entertained by Indian displays and attentions of various kinds', including Indian jugglers.[7] What he saw was so impressive that he later defended earlier travellers' tales, 'stories . . . so new and so incredible to the minds of their readers, that they are set down as positive romances. Marco Polo . . . was, for five hundred years, believed to be an arrant romancer. It is only now, in the nineteenth [century], when we begin to go there ourselves, that we find that Marco, after all, only told things as he saw them.'[8] And one of the things Seward saw would play a small part in the birth of the rope trick legend.

Back in Chicago, Joseph Medill was defeated in the mayoral election by the crime syndicate's candidate and returned to editorship of the *Tribune*. In 1877, Wilkie did indeed follow in his father's footsteps and became a reporter, initially at the *Chicago Times* and then, in 1881, he moved to the *Tribune*. At that time, the two Chicago newspapers were involved in the increasingly aggressive circulation wars of the late nineteenth century. Each paper had once been 'armed and barricaded against an expected assault by the other', and the competition would at times result in violence on the streets between those employed to sell newspapers.[9] In later years, the battle between the Chicago papers would be described as the most violent of the newspaper wars, one from which 'the personnel for Chicago's future gangs was assembled', providing training for 'the system of gang warfare and racketeering' that would expand in the 1920s under Al Capone.[10] But for now, the newspapers fought with words and, on occasion, with the word of God.

In 1881, as Wilkie was switching allegiances, the *Tribune* announced it was to publish the full text of the recent 'Revised New Testament Edition' in a sixteen-page supplement in May of that year. 'No other newspaper in the world will have a standard edition of the New Testament like this one,' it declared, 'a perfect reproduction of the original print, free from typographic or telegraphic errors, and in large type.'[11] The *Chicago Times*, however, sought to scoop its rival by printing 'the principal changes in the Old and New Testaments made by the Committee on Revision' before the *Tribune*'s full text could be printed.[12] Needless to say, this deeply upset the *Tribune*, which denounced 'the fraudulent newspaper' for its 'shallow trick', and pointed out that 'its forgeries in [the] case of the New Testament are now proved by indubitable evidence. A comparison of its fraudulent version with the true version printed this morning [in the *Tribune*] shows that the former is false in nearly every particular.'[13] And having convinced its readers of the fraudulent, false forgeries of its rival, the *Tribune* took some pride in its own work. While it 'was not inclined to boast of its present achievement', it soon managed to overcome modesty, stating that 'it was an epitome of the world's news, both of this world and the world to come . . . It was the most remarkable newspaper ever issued on this continent.'[14]

Throughout the circulation wars, less spiritual topics were also discussed. The *Times* successfully exploited a growing appetite for sensationalist stories, with headlines of 'Sexual Skulduggery', and seems to have had a particular liking for stories about hanging. One article, on the execution of repentant murderers, was memorably entitled 'Jerked to

Jesus'.[15] Meanwhile, the *Tribune* would dismiss its rival's success in the most direct language. 'What can possibly ail that venerable lunatic', it enquired of the *Times*'s editor, 'if not the consciousness of the inferiority of his own newspaper in any respect to the *Tribune?*'[16] To the rising threat from the *Chicago Herald*, on the other hand, the *Tribune* would ponder, 'what does quantity of circulation matter if its character is low?'[17] Yet the *Tribune* was also trying to widen its appeal to a growing audience. By 1890, the census showed Chicago had overtaken Philadelphia to become the nation's second city, and the variety of topics that made the press reflected a more eclectic approach. In August, the *Tribune* discussed a theory 'to improve mankind' by ridding society of 'the drunkard, the insane, the morally weak, and the brutish'. At the end of the discussion, the paper dryly noted that the proponent of this anti-brute theory had failed to explain whether this would be achieved by 'murder, mutilation or imprisonment for life'. That same month, the *Tribune* debated how hydrophobia could be caused by 'an active imagination', disguises worn by Parisian detectives, and there was a story on local women who rode bicycles entitled 'Girls on Wheels'. Before the end of the year, the front page of the *Tribune* was covered with a report on the assassination of Sitting Bull, shot dead while resisting arrest on the morning of 16 December 1890, a man they described as 'the most crafty Indian of modern times'.

We do not know whether Wilkie was responsible for any of these articles, but we do know of one that he wrote at this time. It was also a story about crafty Indians, but he was not referring to the Sioux. It appeared in the midst of more mundane topics, sandwiched between an article complaining of the recent drought, and another on a scheme to pipe water into the Chicago area from Lake Superior. And it launched the greatest legend of the Orient.

The article, which was written anonymously, was about two men. Fred S. Ellmore was a local Chicagoan, a Yale man of '86 with an interest in photography. George Lessing had been a classmate, and was a keen amateur artist. Both had travelled widely and had recently returned from India, where they had seen some quite extraordinary things. They had seen a fakir place a mango seed in a bowl, and had watched as it had grown into a small tree. They had seen the very same fakir place a baby beneath a shawl, cut and slash at the infant with a knife, then remove the shawl to show that the baby had mysteriously gone. And then they had seen the finale:

> The fakir drew from under his knee a ball of gray twine. Taking the loose end between his teeth he, with a quick upward motion, tossed the ball into the air. Instead of coming back to him it kept on going up and up until out of sight and there remained only the long swaying end. . . . [A] boy about

six years old ... walked over to the twine and began climbing it . . . The boy disappeared when he had reached a point thirty or forty feet from the ground . . . A moment later the twine disappeared.

The men, however, had been prepared for this. They had heard of the miraculous feats of Indian jugglers, and were keen to discover their secret. Fred, with his faithful Kodak in hand, had taken photographs. Beside him, George, with pencil and paper, had made sketches of what he had seen. Later, Fred had developed the photographs and compared them with the sketches, and there, right in front of him, was the secret. A sketch showing a boy climbing up the twine, and a photograph, taken at the same time, showing no such thing. No twine, no boy, only the fakir sitting on the ground. There was the explanation of the miracle, 'Mr Fakir had simply hypnotised the entire crowd, but he couldn't hypnotise the camera.' The evidence relating to this important discovery was to be forwarded to the SPR in London, and the article ended by noting that '[t]he report from the London society will be awaited with much interest'.[18] And with that, the anonymous writer of the article sent the story to press, along with sketches of the fakir's feats, and wondered whether anyone would take notice of it.

The next day it was on the front page of the *Tribune*.[19] Over the following weeks, the story reappeared in America and Britain, and it was not long before it had been 'translated into well-nigh every European language'.[20] Four months later, it had provoked so much discussion that a professor wrote to the *Tribune* hoping to clarify matters. The professor, a proponent of hypnosis, complained of sceptics who refused to believe the story was real, and demanded the editor of the *Tribune* 'silence their folly by an assurance of the truth'. The *Tribune* was left with little choice but to come clean. After all, Fred had not really seen a boy climb up a twine and disappear, or even thought he had seen it happen. No sketches had been made and no photographs had been taken. Fred had never been to India, or anywhere else for that matter. Fred did not exist, except in the fertile imagination of the anonymous writer. With some trepidation, no doubt, the *Tribune* published a retraction admitting the story of four months earlier had been a hoax,

> written for the purpose of presenting a theory in an entertaining form. The writer believed that hypnotism might be the secret of the art of the Indian jugglers. [But it] seems that a number of people who read the article in the *Tribune* and in the exchanges that copied it accepted it as a solemn fact.[21]

The author of the story was not named but, according to the *Tribune*'s retraction, the name of the key character – Fred

IT IS ONLY HYPNOTISM.

HOW INDIAN FAKIRS DECEIVE THOSE
WHO WATCH THEM.

Fred S. Ellmore, a Young Chicagoan, Dem-
onstrates the Truth of His Theory at
Gaya, India

'. . . a boy about six years old . . .
walked over to the twine and began
climbing it . . .'

'The boy disappeared . . . A
moment later the twine
disappeared.'

The headline, sketches and some of the copy from the original *Chicago
Daily Tribune* story. And so a legend was born.

S. Ellmore – had been intended as a clue to the reader that the story was a 'sell'. We are fortunate to have the genuine explanation available, as a cynic might mistakenly assume that the name, Fred S. Ellmore, suggests another reason for the story: to 'sell more' newspapers.

This admission might well have been the end of the matter, had it been read by those who had seen the original story, but it seems that few were even aware of it. Indeed, it might well have been lost for ever, and the author of the story would never have been known, but for Andrew Stewart. Stewart, editor of a popular British weekly, *People's Friend*, had read various copies of the original story, and wrote to the editor of the *Tribune* for more information. Though he later claimed to have immediately suspected a hoax, he also wrote a letter to the fictitious Fred S. Ellmore. The editor of the *Tribune* passed this on to the author of the story, as yet unnamed, who replied directly to Stewart with an explanation similar to the one published in the *Tribune*, adding: 'I am led to believe . . . that the little story attracted more attention than I dreamed it could, and that many accepted it as perfectly true. I am sorry that any one should have been deluded.' And the letter was signed, with no obvious sense of irony, 'sincerely yours, John E. Wilkie'.[22]

Wilkie's little story had certainly attracted attention. According to Stewart, 'it was very soon made apparent that the article had found not only believers in its authenticity but that numerous papers and journals were doing their utmost to disseminate the hoax and to make as many believe in it as possible'. Nevertheless, the people's friend was optimistic that he had now resolved the matter. 'It pricks the bladder completely', he declared with metaphorical enthusiasm, 'and lets out the gas that has been generated on the subject. We have been enabled to explode a pernicious hoax.'[23]

The bladder had been pricked, perhaps, but despite Stewart's explosion, much gas remained. For Wilkie's signed confession was never given a fraction of the publicity his original story received, and while he would quickly be forgotten, his story would not. John Nevil Maskelyne did not mention Wilkie, but quickly recognised this 'most ingenious little story' as a good example of the 'Genesis of Oriental miracles'. Such an invention was, for Maskelyne, typical of a 'source to which, no doubt, a few of the supposed wonders of the East may be traced', and with a degree of foresight added, '[n]o doubt we shall find it cropping up from time to time in the most unexpected places'.[24]

Richard Hodgson of the SPR, who had done so much to damage the reputation of Madame Blavatsky, was equally sceptical. The society, of course, had not received any evidence from Ellmore, and Hodgson informed fellow members that the *Tribune* article was the source of the recent batch of stories in the press, and that it had been a hoax. He did not credit Wilkie either, but instead noted that '[t]he story of the boy climbing the rope and disappearing is, in one form or another, very old'.[25] This would be another reason why Wilkie would not be remembered as the man who launched the legend. For while he was responsible for making the story famous, the story itself was not entirely original. There had been, for centuries, many stories of ropes, cords, chains and the like rising into the air, of humans and animals climbing to the top and disappearing. Such stories, in fact, can be found in the mythologies and folklore of several cultures, not only in India but in Europe and China, in North America and Australia. There is, therefore, nothing intrinsically Indian about them. For a legend of an Indian rope trick to take off, it was necessary for such a story to be popularly associated with India, and that is what Wilkie achieved, whether he intended to or not. It was only later that these earlier tales, some from India, but most of them from elsewhere, came to be recognised as versions of the by-then-famous Indian rope trick. We shall see later how this happened, and how it resulted in Wilkie's role being lost in a maze of invented history. But where did Wilkie himself get the idea from?

One possibility was Ibn Battuta, that delicate Moroccan who had reported a levitating cube at the court of Delhi in the fourteenth century, and who had subsequently fainted. Ibn Battuta had also written of a juggler who:

took a wooden ball, with several holes in it through which long thongs were passed, and (laying hold of one of these) slung it into the air. It went so high that we lost sight of it altogether . . . There now remained only a little of the end of a thong in the conjuror's hand, and he desired one of the boys who assisted him to lay hold of it and mount. He did so, climbing by the thong, and we lost sight of him also!

Certainly this was a similar story, but it had nothing to do with India, for Ibn Battuta claimed that he saw this in China. And, in any case, it was not the whole story. For after the boy vanished:

> [t]he conjuror then called to him three times, but getting no answer he snatched up a knife as if in a great rage, laid hold of the thong, and disappeared also! By and bye [*sic*] he threw down one of the boy's hands, then a foot, then the other hand, and then the other foot, then the trunk, and last of all the head! Then he came down himself, all puffing and panting, and . . . took the lad's limbs, laid them together in their places, and gave a kick, when, presto! there was the boy got up and stood before us![26]

And after this somewhat gruesome finale to the Chinese thong trick, Ibn Battuta had fainted.

A similar story had been told by Edward Melton, an Anglo-Dutch traveller of the seventeenth century, though he had not mentioned India either, rather he had reported it from Batavia (present-day Jakarta). There was, as we have seen earlier, a tale from India, one of many from the memoirs of Emperor Jahangir, but he had written of a chain, not a rope or twine, and of animals, not a juggler. It so happens, however, that all of these stories had been translated into English in the nineteenth century, and had been gathered together in 1873 by Colonel Henry Yule. Yule published a new edition of Marco Polo's travels and, in a footnote to the section on China, had noted these stories bore a striking resemblance.[27] The book was a popular one, but it was of two substantial volumes, and even those who read both of them could have been forgiven for missing this footnote. Those who did read the footnote, however, would have naturally associated the stories, as the editor had, with China. Certainly, when John Nevil Maskelyne, that authority on Indian jugglers, wrote of the stories at this time, he referred to them as Chinese.[28]

But we know of two people who did read this footnote, and both of them had a particular interest in India. The first was Colonel Henry Olcott, a keen student of the occult, and a close associate of the second, the enigmatic Madame Blavatsky. According to Colonel Olcott, Madame Blavatsky had seen a similar feat. She had not seen it in India either, in fact she had probably not seen it at all, but she claimed to have seen it in Egypt. A rope had not been used either, but 'a huge roll of tape, that might be twelve or eighteen inches wide'. The juggler had 'flung it straight up into the air. Instead of falling back to earth after it had ascended a short distance, it kept on upward, unwinding and unwinding interminably from the stick, until it grew to be a mere speck, and finally passed out of sight.' Not to be outdone, Blavatsky had gone on to tell how a boy had climbed the tape and disappeared, and how a bloody dismemberment of the boy had followed. Colonel Olcott had subsequently written of Blavatsky's Egyptian tape trick, and had compared it to Ibn Battuta's Chinese thong trick. But then he had made a further comparison, one with a recent account from India. It was an account from William H. Seward, Lincoln's former opponent, and the old enemy of the editor of the *Tribune*. Olcott declared:

> I have seen it stated in the papers that the late William H. Seward, ex-Secretary of State, witnessed a similar feat in India, while on his tour around the world. He saw a man climb up a pole sixty feet high, standing in open air, and when he reached the top he disappeared.[29]

Perhaps this connection was all Madame Blavatsky needed to link these various stories from around the world to India, as far as she was concerned the home of magic. At some point over the following months, as she was writing her two volumes of *Isis Unveiled*, she decided to include some of these stories. For the most part, she simply plagiarised what had been written in Yule's *The Book of Ser* [sic] *Marco Polo*, and argued that this was an example of maya, the Hindu concept of the world as an illusion, where miracles are possible because the real world of experience is not in fact real. The title she gave to this short section of her long book was 'The Indian tape-climbing trick an illusion'. Here, perhaps, are the roots of Wilkie's story about an illusion of a twine rising in the air, of a boy climbing the twine and disappearing, an illusion that never really happened, and one that never really happened in India. In 1877, of course, these roots were little known, lost in two large volumes of esoteric ambiguity. But those who took an interest in psychic matters knew of Blavatsky's writings, and when they read Wilkie's article years later, they quickly made the connection.[30] Yet it seems unlikely that Wilkie would have made such a connection, for there is nothing to suggest he had an interest in the esoteric writings of Theosophists. It seems rather that somebody else supplied him with the idea, and that man could hardly have been better qualified.

Harry Kellar was, at the end of the nineteenth century, America's most popular magician. Yet he had begun his career in conjuring as a boy assistant to the Fakir of Ava. He had worked for several years as agent and business manager of the Davenport brothers, and had gone on to perform his own version of their spirit cabinet, this time as a demonstration of fake spiritualism. He was also familiar not only with India, but also with certain extraordinary phenomena that were reported there, and seems to have held an ambivalent view about such events. In Calcutta, for example, Kellar had attended a seance with a spirit medium, and had concluded that the phenomena were 'in no way the result of trickery', but had later claimed to be able to 'duplicate any performance given by mediums of whatever nature'.[31] He had also maintained that feats of Indian juggling had 'baffled my deepest scrutiny, and remained the inexplicable subject of my lasting wonder and admiration', yet had also stated that 'the ability of the entire fraternity of Indian jugglers is beneath contempt'. Inconsistencies such as these led Richard Hodgson of the SPR to suggest that Kellar's memory was 'not very good'.[32] This interesting combination of a dubious memory with an interest in both spiritualism and India, and the fact that he had been in India at the same time as Madame Blavatsky and Colonel Olcott, may explain the story that he had told on his return home. In 1886, Kellar had published a book about his travels, and had written a chapter about Indian jugglers. Of a story he had heard, he had announced that:

the writers who declare that they have seen such impossible feats performed, as throwing a ball of twine in the air to form a sort of Jack-in-the-beanstalk up which the juggler climbed out of sight, and that the pistol shot of a companion conjuror brought the ariel [*sic*] climber to earth in fragments, which, when brought together, became a living, uninjured man again, must have had their brains steeped in hasheesh.[33]

Kellar's book was published in Wilkie's home town of Chicago, and the form of Kellar's story suggests that this is where Wilkie's idea of a trick with a 'ball of twine' came from. Yet Wilkie had written of hypnosis not hashish, and that part of his story most likely came from London. Since Wilkie's fictitious Fred S. Ellmore had offered to send his evidence to the SPR, Wilkie was obviously aware his theory would interest them. And interest them it certainly did. For just before his article came out, the SPR had been discussing the idea that feats of Indian juggling might be illusions, the result of collective hypnosis. Some even thought it might finally explain the otherwise inexplicable feats of D.D. Home, who had died recently and left behind a unique legacy of mystery. There had, in fact, already been a story about an Indian juggler who had allegedly caused his audience to have a collective hallucination. The *Journal* of the SPR remarked: 'if this story be true, and if Home, like this juggler, had the power of suggesting hallucinations – without any process of hypnotisation – to sane and healthy witnesses, this would certainly take us a long way further in explaining the records with which we have to deal'.[34]

It was out of this late Victorian interest in psychic phenomena and the feats of Indian jugglers, and no doubt inspired at some level by the writings of Theosophists about Chinese thongs and Egyptian tapes, that the legend of the Indian rope trick was born. It may have been conceived by the union of Harry Kellar's accusation of drug abuse and the SPR's interest in collective hypnosis, but Wilkie's story was not quite like any of the earlier lesser-known tales – there was no bloody finale, no animals, and it was firmly located in India. In those respects, it was similar to the story told by that old enemy of Wilkie's editor, William H. Seward. But unlike its older relations, Wilkie's story rapidly spread far and wide, reaching a larger audience than any of its predecessors. Thanks to Wilkie, a story about an Indian rope trick, as it came to be called, had entered the popular imagination of the West, and had begun its rise to legendary status.

For the moment, however, there was no legend, merely a well-known story about an Indian rope trick, and in the first few years that story was being dismissed as a travellers' tale. In 1892, the *Graphic* magazine accepted the reality of many Indian juggling feats, but not this one, pointing out that '[s]ome of the marvels popularly attributed to Indian jugglers – as, for instance, the rope thrown into the air, up which the juggler climbs and disappears – are obviously mere romance, and not worth serious discussion'.[35] Such dismissals made for a bleak future, made bleaker still by the fact that the younger generation were being told to dismiss the story as well. The *Boy's Own Paper* described to its young readers stories of the rope trick, but the writer explained to his impressionable audience:

> Many stories like this I have heard, but never have I met a man who saw such a feat with his own eyes. It was always someone else who had told him that somebody he knew knew some other fellow, who vouched for the truthfulness of the man who had seen it! But where witnesses can be named, and time and place given, stories of wondrous deeds have to be treated as worthy of credence.[36]

Without first-hand, eye-witness accounts, the story of the rope trick had little chance of long-term survival. Nevertheless, Wilkie must have been pleased: pleased that by 1899, less than a decade after he had written the story, the *Strand Magazine* was presenting the rope trick as the most famous feat of the most celebrated representatives of the greatest possession of the largest empire in the world; and pleased that, with the exception of a few people with a particular interest in psychic matters, nobody seemed to be holding him responsible. A few years later, he may have been sitting at home, reading the *Chicago Sunday Examiner*, in which the great English conjuror Charles Bertram categorically dismissed the trick as a myth. 'As for the rope trick,' he said with great authority, he had 'heard of men who had heard of others who had seen it, but I could get no direct evidence', and he concluded that '[t]here is no such trick . . . All in imagination, all in travellers' tales.'[37] So it was that the story was being blamed on the boasts of travellers, and was gradually dying from lack of first-hand evidence. Wilkie, with a mixture of relief and regret, must have thought it was all over. In a short time, a tall tale about a boy and a rope had risen to international fame, but its fall now seemed inevitable. One can only imagine what he must have felt when the story was saved by an extraordinary turn of events, when travellers' tales and first-hand evidence came to the rescue of the tale they had threatened to destroy. A few years after he had told his story of a rope that rose in the air, of a boy that climbed up and disappeared, visitors to India began to come forward claiming to have seen the trick for themselves.

5

A New Tale from India

'I, Sebastian Thomas Burchett, of No. 31 Westcroft Square, Ravenscroft Park, witnessed the Indian rope-climbing trick.' S. T. Burchett was a gentleman of twenty-four, and was described as 'absolutely honest'. He was known to a member of the SPR, whose *Journal* had been discussing the topic for some time now. On 19 March 1904, he received a visit from an SPR investigator in order to take a signed statement:

> The audience stood in a circle round an open space, in the centre of which the conjurer stood. There were no trees near. The rope was in a coil on the ground. The conjurer then got hold of a small boy, and said something to him in Hindustani. The boy then began to climb the rope, hand over hand, with

legs twisted round the rope in the ordinary way of climbing. When he got to the top the boy disappeared. One seemed to be gradually aware that he had disappeared, but not able to fix the exact moment of disappearance.[1]

Despite the numerous claims that have been made since, that the Indian rope trick has been around for centuries, it was not until the twentieth century that an eye-witness reported seeing the rope trick in India. The wonderful century was over, the Victorians were gone, and the story of the rope trick might well have joined them had it not been valiantly rescued by this respectable gentleman in Edwardian London.[2] Heroes, of course, are rarely perfect, and S. T. Burchett was heroic in that sense. He had seen the trick in '1900 or 1901, I do not recollect', he could not 'give the names of any European witnesses who were present', and having signed the above statement in front of witnesses from the SPR, he then went on to change his story the very next day. There were, in the view of the SPR investigators, 'several discrepancies between Mr Burchett's earlier and later accounts', and our hero admitted he had got 'somewhat mixed up'. Faced with these inconsistent details, the investigators concluded that this 'illustrates once more the unreliability of memory with regard to such incidents as these'. But for all the messy details, the main points of the story were consistent. He had seen in India a rope rise into the sky, a boy climb the rope and disappear, and he bravely stated this publicly, albeit in slightly different ways. In doing so, he set an example that was to be followed by others.

A few months later, a second eye-witness came forward, but this time asked to remain anonymous. Reading this lady's account in the SPR *Journal*, it is not hard to understand why:

> One of them threw a rope into the air which hitched itself up to apparently nothing in the sky above; one could see the rope going straight up as far as one could see anything . . . A small boy then swarmed up this rope, becoming smaller and smaller, till he likewise vanished from sight, and a few minutes later bits of his (apparently mangled) remains fell from the sky, first an arm, then a leg, and so on till all his component parts had descended; these the juggler covered with a cloth, mumbled something or other, made a pass or two, and behold! there was the boy smiling and whole before us.

When Ibn Battuta had seen something similar in China, he had, characteristically, fainted. This British lady was made of sterner stuff, however, and dryly remarked that the 'performance did not rouse any particular comment'. Nevertheless, her reluctance to put her name to her account does suggest she expected others might have some sort of comment, and they did. Yet it was surprisingly open-minded.

The *Magazine of Magic* described this version of the rope trick to its readership of conjurors, and claimed that it had been 'vouched for by men of unimpeachable reputation'. In fact, it had been vouched for by one anonymous lady, but a legend does not survive on accuracy. The *Magazine* further pointed out that 'magicians know [the rope trick] cannot be achieved by magical art, as we understand it', and asked, 'what then is the explanation?' And their willingness to accept the story was matched by their willingness to accept an explanation they had heard of, 'one that has been supported strongly in the press'. Vaguely aware of the newspaper story that had launched the legend, but clearly unaware that it had been a hoax, the *Magazine* explained that the trick had been photographed, that the developed photographs 'afterwards showed absolutely no record of the trick', and concluded that the trick was the result of a 'hypnotic vision'.[3] Shortly afterwards, Walter Gibson, a well-known though not always well-informed magician, was spreading this message further afield. He described this version of the rope trick in the *Johannesburg Star*, and told its readers that 'the hypnotic explanation [for it] has been authentically recorded'.[4] If those claiming expertise in magic accepted this more gruesome version of the rope trick, and its accompanying explanation of collective hypnosis, others not versed in the secrets of the art would no doubt have gone along with their expert assessment of the situation. But the situation was about to change and, as a result, this rope trick would barely get off the ground. It would return in years to come, and would rise to prominence as the official rope trick, but for the moment it would have to wait.

Meanwhile, the whole nature of Anglo-Indian relations was changing. Indian leaders had supported the British in the Great War, expecting this would lead to a substantial transfer of power in India, but they were to be disappointed. And it was in the aftermath of the Amritsar Massacre of 1919, when a British colonel opened fire on a peaceful protest and killed hundreds of unarmed men, women and children, that Gandhi began his policy of non-cooperation. Yet, in the midst of these profound political developments, a quite different topic of debate was hitting the headlines. That same year, the *Daily Mail* was being 'inundated with correspondence about this much-discussed Indian rope trick', and this debate was increasingly splitting into two camps: those who felt they had seen a genuine trick; and those who argued it must be the result of hypnosis. The former position was passionately represented by a sergeant of the East Surrey regiment, recently returned from India, who had seen a man throw up the rope, and 'clearly saw the end of the rope up there above. Then one of the lads swarmed hand over hand up the rope till he reached the top. I saw it, I tell you! . . . I saw it all happen. And I should like to see any conjurers in England do the same.' The alternative position was represented in the same week by Arthur Pegge of Essex, who told how his late brother had taken photographs during a performance of the rope trick, but these had later revealed the conjuror squatting on the ground with the rope lying beside him. 'This,' Arthur humbly suggested, 'supports the theory of hypnotism.' That same day and with somewhat less humility, S. W. Clarke, a senior member of the Magic Circle and editor of the *Magic Circular*, supported the latter view that the rope trick had not been performed, and cited the theory of hallucination.[5]

What readers of the *Daily Mail* thought about this one can only imagine. On one side were those who stated categorically that they had seen the trick with their own eyes; on the other side were those who claimed the witnesses had not seen the trick at all, but only thought they had. And this latter group, whose theory was based on a hoax story, and whose only supporting evidence was a few photographs of nothing happening, seemed to be winning the argument. During the *Daily Mail* debate, the *Magic Circular* published 'unembellished notes of tricks' by a man who had resided for many years in India. 'All the things I have seen in the East', he wrote, 'I divide into two categories: (1) Pure tricks with a reasonable explanation for how they are done, and (2) Hypnotism pure and simple. Scientific men have assured me that it is as easy to hypnotise a crowd as one or two.' Armed with this scientific assurance, and supported by a personal acquaintance who had a photograph which 'showed nothing', he too confidently assured his readers that the rope trick was 'merely hypnotism'.[6] But the proponents of the hypnosis hypothesis were in for a surprise. For the impossible illusion that could only be explained by hypnosis, the illusion that could not be photographed, was about to be shattered. In early 1919, the *Strand Magazine* proudly published 'The Great Indian Rope Trick Photographed for the First Time'.

The man who photographed 'the most famous and the most discussed of any juggling performance in the world' was Lieutenant F. W. Holmes, VC, MM.[7] The venue had been Kirkee, near Poona, and the year had been 1917. An old man had begun 'by unwinding from about his waist a long rope, which he threw upwards in the air, where it remained erect. The boy climbed to the top, where he balanced himself, as seen in the photograph, which I took at that moment. He then descended . . . I offer no explanation,' though he could not resist pointing out that 'this, I think, proves there is no question of hypnotism'.[8]

In response to this challenge to the hypnosis hypothesis, the Chairman of the Magic Circle wrote to the *Daily Mail* to announce a forthcoming meeting to discuss the evidence. Lieutenant Holmes was invited to attend, and to bring his photograph for examination. The meeting was to be held at the Magic Circle headquarters in Anderton's Hotel, Fleet Street, but in view of the great interest in the rope trick, the meeting would be open to the public. Prior to the meeting, the *Magic Circular* noted that 'several hundreds of visitors have asked to be allowed to be present', and given this 'large and influential audience', members were requested to arrive in evening dress 'to give a good impression'.[9] In front of a crowded but well-dressed meeting, Lieutenant Holmes exhibited his photograph, and reiterated what he had told the press. It was a direct challenge to the position that the trick had never been performed, that it was the result of hallucination or hypnosis. This was the theory favoured by several magicians, and the one cited by the editor of the *Magic Circular*, S. W. Clarke. But there in the Magic Circle headquarters, where anything was possible, it was seen 'to support Mr Clarke's theory'. The explanation behind this mysterious transformation was that Mr Clarke had another theory.

This was a much better theory, and did not involve hypnosis. In fact, Magic Circle members, who had recently been given a scientific assurance about how easy it was to hypnotise a crowd, were now told by an expert in hypnosis that the trick 'could not be accounted for on the theory of hypnotism, as it has been proved beyond doubt that a crowd could not be hypnotised'. According to Mr Clarke, Lieutenant Holmes's photograph showed a boy 'balanced on top of a rigid rope or pole', and such a feat hardly required hypnosis.[10] The Lieutenant had already publicly stated that the juggler 'had no pole – a thing that would have been impossible of concealment',[11] so the question was how did the rope stand

The infamous Holmes photograph. Holmes told how the rope was unwound, thrown upwards and remained rigid, stating: 'I offer no explanation.'

in the air and remain erect? Mr Clarke had a theory on that as
well, but as it turned out, it was to prove unnecessary. Later,
we discover that Lieutenant F. W. Holmes, VC, MM, privately
confessed: he had never actually seen the rope rise in the air
and, when subsequently questioned by Mr Clarke, he
admitted there had never been a rope. He had merely seen a
boy balancing at the top of a bamboo pole, and had taken a
picture of it.[12] Mr Clarke seems to have felt no need to
publicly expose the otherwise respectable officer. The rope
trick had been substantially cut down to size, and one no
longer had to invoke the dubious theory of collective hypnosis
for what was left of it. Having now resolved the matter, Mr
Clarke sat back and enjoyed the rest of the evening, in which
'Mr Max Templeton manipulated billiard balls with very great
skill . . . and a Lady Associate of the Magic Circle confirmed
the favourable impression previously made, by some graceful
productions and transformations of eggs and handkerchiefs.'[13]

But the matter was far from resolved. The first ever
photograph of the world's most famous illusion may have been
fake, but only a handful of people knew this. The newspapers,
who had enthusiastically published the photograph, said
nothing of the confession. If the question of the rope trick's
existence arose, and it arose many times, somebody regularly
pointed out that the camera never lied, but nobody ever
suspected the photographer. As a result, the Holmes
photograph remained for many definitive proof that the rope

trick was real. And if the rope trick was real, then it could be found again, and so the search began. At the head of the queue were magicians, most of whom were unaware of Holmes's confession, and were eager to add the most famous of illusions to their repertoire. So it was that a legend born of an American hoax, and reified by a British lie, fooled experts in deception into searching all over India for a secret that was not there. And there it was that these experts in deception found it.

6

The Search for the Secret

'Mr Frank McNaughton is now back from his travels in the East,' the London press announced in 1922, 'whither he sailed last October in search of the elusive Indian rope trick.' It had been a long and difficult quest for Frank, and not without disappointment. Prompted by the reports of witnesses, but not satisfied with them, he had gone in search of what he had only heard of, and had found what he already knew. His 'first investigations were made in Ceylon . . . He then travelled all through Bengal, spending a month in the indigo districts of Tirhoot.' But all he had managed to find was 'a European who gave his word that 15 years back he had seen the rope trick'. He had, however, continued to search for something more tangible. 'I made all possible inquiries in Burma,' he wrote, '[and] on arrival at Bhano, a distance of 1,012 miles up the Irrawaddy river, and practically on the

Chinese border, I met a native who assured me that he had seen the trick.' The word of a European and the assurance of a native, these had been the highlights of his seven-month search for the rope trick, yet his confidence had not been dented. 'I am more confident than ever', he declared, 'that the performance . . . has never been done.' Frank, it seems, had embarked upon a seven-month quest, and travelled thousands of miles across the subcontinent, in search of a trick he was already confident did not exist. A man this optimistic was bound to draw a positive conclusion from a negative experience, and so his opinion, based on the word of a European and the assurance of a native, was that 'on certain rare occasions individuals have been hypnotized into thinking they have seen the performance done'.[1]

Carl Hertz, on the other hand, held a quite different opinion. Hertz was a well-known and successful American illusionist, who had toured the world with his elaborate stage show. In India, he had engaged the Novelty Theatre, Bombay, at a time when the plague was killing five hundred people a day. In the same year that Frank set off on his confident quest, Hertz told of his own attempts to find the rope trick.

> I have long sought the secret . . . I have probed deeply into the literature and tradition which surrounds Indian magic . . . I have toured all over India . . . I have gone off the beaten track and made expeditions to remote districts to try

to see the trick performed . . . I have myself asked scores of
fakirs to perform the trick for me.

The fakirs, however, had not performed the trick for him.
But perhaps they had remembered what had happened last
time. Eager to witness the wonders of India, Hertz had
previously 'gathered fakirs from far and near to give their
exhibitions . . . and, when their performances were over, I
told them, through the interpreter, that I was very displeased
with the childish things which I had seen'. Yet if Hertz lacked
certain diplomatic skills, he cannot be accused of lacking
determination. Later, the man who had performed in the face
of the plague was being praised by the London press for having
mystified audiences 'with the greatest feat of all – the Indian
rope trick – which he claims that he is the only one to produce
with a near approach to the skill of the Hindu fakir'.[2] Had
Hertz finally found the secret to an illusion that many were
confident, and none more than Frank, had never been
performed?

Not if we are to believe Major Branson, whose amateur
conjuring experience was supplemented by the authority of a
man who had been a colonial officer in India since the end of
the Victorian era. In that same year in which Frank announced
his conclusions based on seven months of searching, Major
Branson published a book in which he described his twenty-
three-year search for the rope trick. Throughout that period,

A Carl Hertz poster illustrates how much he impressed the natives.

he had interrogated countless jugglers, and offered to pay a substantial reward to anyone capable of performing the rope trick. For twenty-three years, however, there had been not a single taker, and he concluded, as Frank had done, 'that a rope thrown up into the air has not remained suspended in mid-air, nor has any boy ever climbed up it [and] that when at the top he has not disappeared'.[3] In prose that suggests he did not like having his time wasted, he also dismissed the hypnosis theory and any other attempt to defend the existence of the rope trick as 'not worthy of comment'.

Clearly they could not all be right, but perhaps they were all wrong. Horace Goldin, another well-known American illusionist, managed to contradict all of them when he claimed to be 'the only white man in the world to discover the secret'. Goldin claimed to have travelled to 'localities where white men had never been', and had finally found a yogi 'who made a practice of hanging head downwards from a tree for days on end'. The man, it transpired, was a 'master of the Indian rope trick which was performed as a sacred and religious rite'. In his bid to discover the secret, Goldin spoke to the holy man, and '[i]mmediately several disciples surrounded me. They produced daggers and made me understand that to speak to the yogi might mean death.' Yet in the face of such danger, Goldin persisted until he had extracted the secret from 'one of the yogi's disciples whom I bribed with money'.[4] Goldin was by no means the last to claim he had finally discovered the secret of the Indian rope trick, or the last to claim he was the only one to do so. Various searches were made, and various secrets found, but what few people realised was that those who were searching for the rope trick were searching for different reasons.

Some, such as Frank, sought in earnest, but others sought to debunk and others to profit. Major Branson was a colonial officer, a representative of the modern West, a proponent of the superiority of Western science over Eastern mysticism, and of Western conjurors over Indian jugglers. Such a man found it difficult to tolerate the idea that India might be the home of real magic, or that Indian jugglers could accomplish what his fellow Western conjurors could not. Major Branson was speaking on behalf of Western science and Western superiority, in defence of the empire. Carl Hertz, on the other hand, was an American magician. When he went in search of the Indian rope trick, he was looking for a new miracle to add to his repertoire, a novel performance to draw in the crowds. And as the greatest illusion of all, the secret of the rope trick would be the ultimate find. He was probably as sceptical as Major Branson about its actual existence, but that did not prevent him from performing the trick. On stage there were many advantages to the open ground, fewer angles to worry about, and overhead support. In fact, he was not the first to perform the rope trick on stage, but what Hertz wanted was to give the impression that this was similar to the rope trick of legend, to claim to be 'the only one to produce [the trick] with a near approach to the skill of the Hindu fakir'. This claim to uniqueness was an important piece of showmanship, but was itself hardly unique. When Horace Goldin claimed to be 'the only white man to discover its secret', he was playing a similar game, and he would later confess that:

> it did not matter at all whether the trick had been performed or not. All I cared for was that it was a widely publicized illusion, and if I could perform it I should reap the profit . . . Having failed to discover anything positive about the famous illusion, I decided that the only course left to me was to invent it myself.[5]

Meanwhile, Howard Thurston, yet another famous American performer, presented the 'World's Most Famous Illusion First Time Out of India'.[6] Major Branson, as an amateur conjuror, understood all this, but it frustrated him that the claims of showmen were clouding what he regarded as a more important issue: the threat to the modern scientific world from the growing reputation of the mystic East. Thus, the ambiguity surrounding the legend was fuelled in part by a sceptical amateur conjuror who claimed that the rope trick could not be performed, and professional conjurors who wanted to give the impression that they could perform it. Perhaps, if these gentlemen had been given time to work

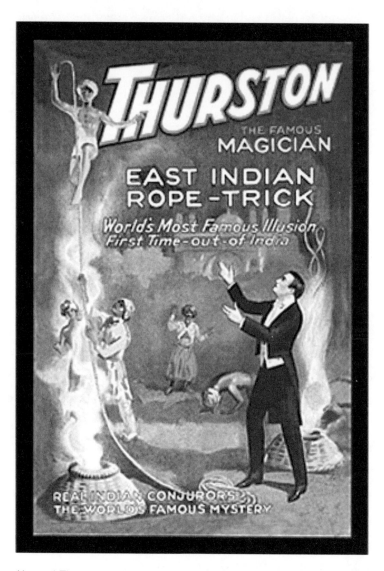

Howard Thurston, once again introducing the rope trick to the West for the first time.

things out, they would have been able to agree that the secret of the rope trick was simple: it could be performed, but only on a stage. Any such gentlemen's agreement, however, was prevented by the memory of a Lady, and the secret of an Earl.

In the aftermath of the various quests of Frank, Carl Hertz and Major Branson, things had been relatively quiet. There had been no eye-witnesses since Lieutenant Holmes had published his photograph of a bamboo pole in 1919, and while Frank's confident suggestion of hypnosis continued to be touted, the competing theories of Hertz and Branson might yet have fused into a compromise. Providing, of course, that there was no more talk of the rope trick being performed in the open air without the advantages of a stage. And then, in 1925, Lady Waghorn made her entrance. In the *Civil and Military Gazette*, she publicly declared she had seen, in an open compound in Madras, a rope 'thrown up into the air, where it remained and a boy of about ten years climbed up it and disappeared'. Lady Waghorn was, of course, married to Lord Waghorn, the etymological roots of whose family name may be speculated upon. But when it came to the Waghorn memory of the rope trick, there was little room for speculation. 'Though it was so many years ago,' she reported, 'in my mind I can distinctly see the whole thing as can also my husband.'[7] It had in fact been thirty-four years since the Waghorns had apparently seen the rope trick. They had not thought it marvellous at the time, they had not mentioned it 'to the butler or any of the other servants', and 'for 34 years she had thought nothing about it'. But the memory of a Waghorn was not to be doubted. 'It was NOT a bamboo the boy climbed,' she replied to an impertinent sceptic, 'IT WAS A ROPE.'[8] Lord Waghorn passed away shortly after his wife's declaration, and though nobody suggested there was a connection, it did leave Lady Waghorn as the sole survivor of the event. Yet the Lady was not for turning. With a confidence in her position that may be peculiar to the British aristocracy, she maintained that she had a 'very reliable memory' of a trick she had not regarded as memorable thirty-four years earlier. The Waghorn declaration prompted others to agree with her and, in the view of the *Civil and Military Gazette*, this was 'sufficient to record the accomplishment of the trick – a point on which there has raged a considerable controversy – and to label the Indian conjuror with a cunning which his Western brother has not succeeded in emulating'.[9]

As a trick that British conjurors could not perform in similar conditions, the existence of the rope trick hurt their professional pride. As an impossible feat that contradicted Western scientific laws it was, for Major Branson, little short of a threat to empire. And it was a threat from within, coming from a member of the British aristocracy. The Waghorn situation was a delicate one, and one that would have to be dealt with by the arrival of a new defender of the sceptical cause. That new defender would also have to deal with the aptly named Sergeant Secrett. Sergeant Thomas Secrett had been aide-de-camp to Earl Haig, the general who had overseen the deaths of so many British soldiers in the Great War that he subsequently set up a fund in their memory, but in his name. Few people who have since bought a poppy realise that Haig allegedly saw the rope trick. Haig himself did not recall the incident. But Sergeant Secrett knew, and in 1929, he revealed all.

It had begun while riding on horseback along a forest road somewhere in the Deccan, that vast plain of Central India. They had seen a fakir, surrounded by a huge crowd, beginning to uncoil a long rope. Haig, a man who could assess a situation quickly and accurately, thought the fakir might be about to perform the rope trick. But as they approached, the fakir stopped what he was doing, and left. Later, to their surprise, he appeared at their bungalow and offered to perform the legendary trick for Haig. He threw the rope into the air, and Haig watched its ascent. The rope immediately fell back to earth, but Haig continued to look upwards. Secrett, whose humble position as Sergeant meant he was not part of the audience, was meanwhile watching from a nearby window. The fakir introduced the boy to his audience, then pointed upwards, and Haig again began to look upwards, as if watching something marvellous. Meanwhile, his faithful Sergeant looked on, wondering what his Commanding Officer was staring at. 'Then the whole thing dawned on me,' he explained, '[the fakir] had mesmerised his audience – including my master!' Secrett, unable to keep one, rushed to the scene of the deception, shouting frantically, 'the boy is still on the ground, sir! . . . and the rope fell the moment he threw it up!' With this abrupt interruption, the spell was broken, and the Sergeant was sure that 'the old fakir was immensely angry with me'. Later that night, he was awoken by a footstep on the balcony outside. Switching on his flashlamp, he saw that, 'coming towards my bed, was a viper, his wicked little eyes glinting in the light'. Reluctant to disturb his master, but seeing the viper dart its head forward, the Sergeant grabbed his revolver, fired, 'and blew half its head off'. This attempt at revenge appears to have provoked in the Sergeant a certain animosity towards fakirs, whom he later described as beggars, a group of Indian society of which he was not particularly fond. 'They simply beg – for no other reason than they want something,' he informed his readers, '[and] I never yet saw an Indian beggar who could not convince a Greek Jew with Scotch blood in his veins that he was deserving!'[10]

Such were the witnesses who helped build the legend of the Indian rope trick. Supported by testimony from a well-connected and resentful sergeant, the hypnosis theory seemed to be in good hands. Meanwhile, the existence of a genuine rope trick rested upon that most solid of foundations: the Waghorn memory. Those who wanted to kill off the legend would have to do something, and none were keener to do so than sceptical Western conjurors. Their professional pride resented the idea that Indian jugglers could perform a trick they regarded as impossible. And their scepticism rested upon the immutable laws of Western science that defined the very limits of what was possible. The Indian rope trick, without the advantages of a stage setting, was impossible, and Indian jugglers could not perform the impossible. People needed to be made to understand this, and the message required a new messenger. So it was that a new hero would emerge to defend the sceptical cause, and a new challenge would be issued. The challenge would be directed at anyone who sought to promote the legend of the rope trick, and the sceptics were confident it would not be accepted. The sceptics, however, were about to be proved wrong.

7

The Magic Circle Challenge

(London, 1933)

Lieutenant Colonel Robert Henry Elliot, MD, FRCS was the most respectable of gentlemen. He was an internationally respected ophthalmologist, a former Hunterian Professor of the Royal College of Surgeons, and a past Chairman of the Naval and Military Committee of the British Medical Association. To those who did not know him well, there was certainly nothing to suggest that the retired eye surgeon, late of the Indian Medical Service, and presently residing at 54 Welbeck Street, London, W1, was particularly mysterious. Some might have known that he was a member of the Magic Circle. But few would have known that within that secretive society was a select group of gentlemen, whose responsibility it was to examine that most esoteric of subjects, the occult.

FOR PRIVATE CIRCULATION ONLY

THE MAGIC CIRCULAR.

A Monthly Review of the Magic Art.

Vol. 23.	MAY, 1929.	No. 264.

Some Prominent Members of the Magic Circle.

LIEUT. COLONEL R. H. ELLIOT, M.I.M.C.

The Chairman of the Occult Committee of the Magic Circle,
keeping a low profile.

This mysterious group was known by those who knew of it as the Occult Committee of the Magic Circle, and those who knew of it knew that its Chairman was a retired eye surgeon, late of the Indian Medical Service. But many more would soon know of Elliot and his Committee, and would watch with wonder as they battled with a legend.

The process of revelation began with Lady Waghorn. Elliot had read of her claims to have seen the impossible rope trick, and realised that they had to be dealt with. As a man of science and a former colonial officer, Elliot might be seen as a graduate of the Major Branson school of thought. India was, in his view, a superstitious and primitive land, and 'if British rule were withdrawn, India would go back without hesitation to hook-swinging and suttee'.[1] As for the Indian rope trick, the existence of an impossible feat was a challenge to the authority of Western science, and the notion that Indian jugglers could perform what Western conjurors could not was an insult to his fellows. The Waghorn situation therefore required firm action, and this was taken when he wrote to the Lady in 1933 and politely invited her to visit his W1 residence in order to discuss her experience. There it was that the Waghorn memory was confronted by members of the Occult Committee, and the discussion that followed might best be described as a battle of wits with an unarmed opponent. That the 'absolute defiance of natural law' had not impressed her was, she admitted, 'incredible'. That nobody had bothered to discuss the event was, she agreed, 'most extraordinary'. She offered no explanation for the fact that she had written nothing down until thirty-four years after the event, or for the fact that nobody else had reported seeing the trick around that time, replying only that it was indeed 'very extraordinary'.

Nevertheless, the Waghorn memory was 'very reliable'. Asked to describe the event again, she claimed that the rope had disappeared at the end of the trick. When it was pointed out that she had previously claimed the rope had been coiled up and put away, 'she denied this'. When several of the Committee reminded her that she had definitely said it, she refused to accept this. The Waghorn memory was, she stressed, 'very good on details', though she admitted it was all 'very extraordinary'. In a bid to demonstrate the reliability of the Waghorn memory, she described a performance of the basket trick on the same day, but got several points wrong. When this was put to her, she 'admitted this might be so, but said she had forgotten the details'. And when asked how she could remember the rope trick in such detail when she could not remember the basket trick properly, 'she offered no explanation', though presumably she thought it all rather extraordinary. Elliot's Committee concluded that 'they did not believe that Lady Waghorn saw the Rope Trick or that anyone accustomed to weighing evidence will seriously believe that she did'.[2]

With the Waghorn memory in tatters, the Lieutenant Colonel turned his guns on Sergeant Secrett. With Earl Haig now dead, he wrote to Lady Haig who, unlike Lady Waghorn, had no memory of the rope trick. 'I have never heard my husband speak of the rope trick,' she assured him, and gave him permission to say this publicly.[3] This he took full advantage of by publishing several articles and a book over the following year. He also questioned the Sergeant's honesty in regard to other aspects of the story, dismissing the Sergeant's claim that the fakir had sent his snake to poison him as laughable. For no area of knowledge was hidden from the Chairman of the Occult Committee, and it so happened that Elliot was something of an authority on snakes. He had worked in Edinburgh with the international snake expert, Professor Sir Thomas Fraser, and had published articles on the subject for both specialists and the public.[4] And so he dismissed the Sergeant's story, declaring with great authority, 'I have studied the ways of snakes long and carefully. All of them are stupid animals.'[5] Receiving no reply from the accused, Elliot regarded the case of Sergeant Secrett as closed.

But the case of the rope trick was far from closed. Some men might have rested, but Elliot was on a mission to kill off the legend once and for all. His next assault was the announcement of a meeting to discuss the rope trick, to be held at the Oxford House Theatre, High St, Marylebone. The Magic Circle had, of course, already held a public meeting in

1919 to discuss the rope trick, and their conclusion then had been that the rope trick was successfully discredited. Clearly, they had got that wrong, but this time they would take no chances, and Lieutenant Colonel Elliot, MD, FRCS assembled an impressive team to deal with the rising legend. The meeting would be chaired by the Rt Hon. The Lord Ampthill, GCSI, GCIE (former Viceroy of India and then President of the Magic Circle), with a committee that included the Rt Hon. The Lord Meston, KCSI, LLD (former Governor of the United Provinces, Agra and Oudh), Sir Michael O'Gwyer, GCIE, KCSI (former Lieutenant Governor of the Punjab), and Brigadier General G. S. Elliot, CBE (no relation). The imperial forces gathered and the battleground agreed upon, hostilities would commence on 30 April 1934 at 8 p.m.[6]

There were, of course, those in the Magic Circle who felt the Committee was going too far. One member, Arnold Crowther, sadly complained:

why must we have our dreams shattered? The world would be dull, miserable and intolerable if we believed only what our step-mother Science would have us believe . . . Science is already robbing us of our Romance . . . We all love mystery and many of us would like to possess the mysterious reputation of the fakir, but [instead] we are always trying to expose him as a fraud.[7]

In a heartfelt appeal to the Committee to recognise the worth of wonder in magic, Arnold pleaded, 'let us leave our Indian brothers to be magicians . . . let us keep the mysteries of the Orient, the greatest of which is the Indian Rope Trick'. Arnold's plea was heartily endorsed by a fellow Circle member, Charles Sampson, who joined him in his stance against the forces of dis-enchantment. Courageously admitting that he still liked to believe in 'Wizards and Fairies', Charles gently admonished the Committee for their work to kill off the rope trick. 'It has baffled me completely why such a stand has been taken against it,' he wrote with delicate defiance, 'it has done no one any harm.'[8]

But the imperial forces were not to be halted by cries for appeasement. In a patriotic call to arms, the former Viceroy, Lord Ampthill, pointed out that '[i]t was in accordance with the traditions of English Conjuring to dispel superstitious beliefs', and reaffirmed the intention of the Occult Committee to confront the enemy of English tradition that was the Indian rope trick.[9] Clearly, it was all being taken very seriously, and there were good reasons why. The Occult Committee had been set up for a serious purpose, and the man who had set it up had fought a serious fight against the supernatural. It had been formed in 1914 by John Nevil Maskelyne, that scourge of mediums, Indian jugglers and free toilet access, and its aims were simple: to investigate claims to supernatural power and to expose fraud. Its main targets had been, of course, fraudulent spiritualist mediums, whose continued success had been assisted by the unparalleled grief that had accompanied the Great War. But as long as people persisted in regarding the feats of Indian jugglers as inexplicable, they would always be a potential target of the Committee.

John Nevil Maskelyne had died shortly after setting up the Committee, but it survived to see the legend of the rope trick grow to unacceptable heights. In fact, in a somewhat ironic fashion, it was the Indian rope trick that ensured the survival of the Occult Committee. The Committee had not been active for several years when Elliot began his campaign. It was reappointed by the Council of the Magic Circle in 1933, and its primary target then was the growing legend of the rope trick.[10] The rope trick was, of course, the perfect enemy. Not only was it being seen by some as a supernatural phenomenon, but it gave the appalling impression that Indian jugglers were superior to Western conjurors. Even those Western conjurors who had searched for the rope trick in India, and who had come to slightly different conclusions about whether it could be performed, had all agreed on one thing: Indian jugglers were not capable of anything that a Western conjuror could not do. Carl Hertz had explained that 'the skill of the Indian conjurers is greatly exaggerated, and that they cannot be compared with any of our first-class Western conjurers', and he could only perform the rope trick on stage.[11] Major Branson had sought 'to uphold the reputation of the Western conjurer against the spurious ascendancy of his Eastern confrere', as he dismissed the rope trick reports from India as nonsense.[12] Yet the legend refused to die, and with each new report that the rope trick had been performed, the reputation of Indian jugglers continued in its spurious ascendancy. It was, therefore, the patriotic duty of the Committee, and in the interests of truth and commonsense, to deal with the problem once and for all.

With the imperial forces gathered in the Oxford House Theatre on 30 April 1934, the meeting began at 8 p.m. sharp. Lord Ampthill addressed the audience with 'very appropriate words', and Mr Clarke, editor of the *Magic Circular*, then spoke on the history and origins of the rope trick. These history and origins had nothing to do with John E. Wilkie or the *Chicago Tribune*, but this is a quite distinct strand of confusion that will be dealt with later. Meanwhile, Dr Edwin Smith once again 'disposed of the hypnotic explanation', while Mr Harry Price, a bibliophile, explained that 'not one word of evidence in favour of the trick was to be found in his 12,000 volumes on conjuring'. Elliot then summed up the evidence, allowing him another opportunity to repeat the words of Lady Haig about her husband never having seen the trick, before coming to the conclusion that had always been the point. The rope trick, as reported by witnesses, had never been done and would never be done, and the following challenge was issued to all: 'If anyone will come forward and perform the Indian Rope Trick before my Committee, we will give him 500 guineas. The rope must be thrown into the air and defy the force of gravity, whilst someone climbs up it and disappears.'[13]

The Occult Committee 'were satisfied that the meeting was a great success [and] that it provided the greatest publicity the Magic Circle has ever enjoyed'.[14] The *Magic Circular* concluded, with admirable optimism in light of recent experience, that 'the verdict has relegated this ancient myth to the realm of the non-existent'. The testimony of such 'distinguished men', and the 'cumulative effect of the negative evidence', were felt to be 'overwhelming', and the *Circular* confidently predicted that 'it will be a bold man, or one careless of his reputation for veracity, who in future claims to have seen the most famous trick which has never been performed'.[15] It was, of course, only a matter of days before such a bold and careless man came forward.

He boldly described himself as His Excellency Dr Sir Alexander Cannon, KGCB, MD, DSc., Ph.D, DLitt., DPM, MA, Docteur de l'Université, Professeur et Académicien, VP et Doyen de Sevatus, Académie Internationale, MA, FRSA, FRSM, FRGS, FACP, FRSTM, and Hon. FBPS, Hon. FFA, etc. And if further evidence was required of Dr Cannon's carelessness with his reputation for veracity, it was soon supplied. Dr Cannon's claim was not simply that he had seen the rope trick, but that he could reproduce the illusion on demand. He claimed, in fact, that he could produce the phenomenon of the Indian rope trick in London's largest theatre, the Albert Hall, and his plan was as simple as it was bold. He would invite a yogi over from India to create the illusion in London, but would recreate Indian conditions exactly. He would bring over 'a shipload of special sand, and heat up the Albert Hall to tropical temperature, and produce [his] own tropical lighting'. The Committee, in the interests of public relations, agreed to meet with the Doctor on 9 June 1934 to discuss what one magician called, with relative restraint, 'a ridiculous offer'. Thankfully, the brief highlights of the meeting were recorded in the minutes of the Occult Committee.

Dr Cannon 'arrived in good time, and immediately expressed his willingness to arrange for a demonstration of the rope trick in London for a fee of 50,000 pounds'. The offer, of course, had been 500 guineas, but Dr Cannon felt this 'would be an insult to the yogi he would invite to England. Also the expense would be very great, as a shipload of sand was essential to produce the illusion.' Not to mention the tropical heating of the Albert Hall. The Committee asked, one assumes hypothetically, whether he would give 'a banker's guarantee that the money plus expenses would be returned in the event of failure. The reply was in the negative.' Instead, Dr Cannon 'went deeply into the subject of psychic phenomena', in which the Committee 'considered his claims very extravagant. He maintained that he lived in the fourth dimension, and indicated that it was a sphere foreign to the understanding of the others present.' And on this unexpected point of agreement, Elliot thanked Dr Cannon for his attendance, and the meeting was closed at seven o'clock.[16]

It had certainly been a long day for the Committee. They had already discussed the claims of Professor Bofeys. Bofeys was a member of the International Brotherhood of Magicians, and, according to recent press reports, had performed the Indian rope trick at last year's IBM convention. It was, however, common knowledge among members of the IBM that 'his claim had been a spontaneous joke, but sections of the press had published the item as a matter of fact'. The Committee had therefore written to the relevant newspapers repudiating the Bofeys claim and explaining the true position. But, that day, the secretary had to report that the papers had not replied, and had declined to print the Committee's letter. To those who had already 'relegated the ancient myth to the realm of the non-existent', press reports on its existence were particularly frustrating. All the more so because truth and commonsense did not help sell newspapers. And then there were the continuing claims of some professional conjurors. One of these was Percy Tibbles, though that was not the name he used in public. Percy had, in previous years, performed as an Egyptian, but subsequently decided on a less radical change of image, a rough reversal of his name that resulted in P. T. Selbit. He is little known today outside the world of magic, but the trick he invented remains synonymous with the image of a magician, the most typical trick since Victorian conjurors had begun to pull rabbits from hats. Percy had placed a lady into a large coffin-shaped box and had sawn through her middle.

The idea had been immediately successful and had, therefore, been promptly stolen. Horace Goldin, the American illusionist who claimed to be the first white man to discover the secret of the Indian rope trick, had begun to perform a surprisingly similar trick. Horace, however, had maintained that it was not the same. Percy had 'sawed through a lady', while Horace pointed out with no obvious sense of irony that he 'sawed a lady in half'. While this radical shift certainly caught on, Percy had questioned how radical it was. The two rivals were soon in fierce competition, and when Percy had planned a tour of America, Horace had planned one too, with the advantage of being in America already. By the time Percy was sawing through American ladies, many had already been sawn in half by Horace, and so had the impact of Percy's performance. There was, to say the least, a degree of rivalry between Percy and Horace. So when one responded to the challenge to perform the rope trick, it is hardly surprising that the other did as well. Their responses to the challenge were characteristically similar, with subtle variations. Percy had written to the Committee claiming he could perform the rope trick, and they had replied that 'it must be done in the open, away from houses, trees, or any such construction'. By the Committee meeting of 9 June, 'no further communication had been received'. Horace, on the other hand, had written to the *Morning Post* to accept the challenge. That same day, the Committee 'agreed that as it was not addressed to them in any way, no notice should be taken'. The Committee would be proved correct when Horace later confessed he had made up his various claims about having discovered the secret of the rope trick. Meanwhile, having dealt as well as they could with the spurious claims of the various parties, the Committee might well have relaxed, with the satisfaction characteristic of a good day's work, had Elliot not looked at his watch and realised that 'Dr Cannon is due at 6'.[17]

There was, however, no shortage of curious individuals for Elliot to contend with. Soon, an article appeared in the very respectable *Chambers' Journal*, written by Harold T. Wilkins, who stirred up things that Elliot had thought already settled. Harold T. Wilkins not only spoke up on behalf of the bizarre Dr Cannon, but stated that the rope trick had been performed by Professor Bofeys, whose performance had 'mystified men who know most of the secrets of magic and conjuring'.[18] With no desire to return to the fourth dimension of Dr Cannon, Elliot simply pointed out again that the Professor Bofeys claim had been a practical joke. Harold T. Wilkins responded, in true sceptical fashion, by stating that he would be 'very surprised' if that were the case, and questioning Elliot's accuracy. Once again, and with diminishing patience, Elliot wrote to the press in order to explain the details of the hoax, providing Harold T. Wilkins with the names of those present who could confirm what had happened, and explaining in no uncertain terms that what he had said was accurate. Harold T. Wilkins's bewildering response was to accuse Elliot of not being 'clear as to the precise meaning on various points'. If Elliot's frustration was tested by the end of reading this letter, we can only hope he did not read on, as the next letter was from an elderly gentleman who remembered having seen the rope trick sixty years earlier.[19]

Press coverage continued to confuse matters. A few days after the meeting, the *Daily Telegraph* wrote that 'the Occult Committee has reported that the rope trick is a myth, and that no-one has actually seen it performed'. On the same page, however, were letters from two gentlemen, each claiming to have seen it performed. Elliot wrote to the *Telegraph*, asking them for any corroborating evidence of what they reported, for the names of any other witnesses to this remarkable event, and must have wondered whether the newspaper would even print his letter. The *Telegraph* not only printed it, but printed another immediately below it from a witness who claimed he had also seen the rope trick performed.[20] This can only have frustrated Elliot further, who, perhaps hoping for a more sympathetic ear, wrote to the *Listener*. There, he sought once more to end the debate, but once again prolonged it. Perhaps he was asking for trouble when he referred to the authority of the last Viceroy, Lord Irwin, who had been unable to find the rope trick, and sneered, 'where great people like Lord Irwin have failed, unknown and unimportant members of society claim to have succeeded'.[21] Before long, the *Listener* was being bombarded with letters from unknown and unimportant members of society.

The letters page is that most democratic of forums, open to all and ignored by most. Here is where the voices of those desperate to be heard can cry out to a select audience of people on long journeys who have finished reading the news, and cannot do crosswords. At the end of 1934, however, the opinions of the unknown and unimportant were being expressed on the most high-profile and significant of topics, none more so than the possibility of a future war with Germany. A letter on the 'Causes of War' complained of 'Winston Churchill's voice relentlessly inferring Germany as the imminent aggressor of this country', a position the author regarded as 'essential folly. For no country is more eager for friendship with England than Germany.'[22] The letter, however, was split in half by a photograph of an Indian man sitting on the ground, beside a boy at the top of a vertical rope. For there was a topic of greater interest at this time, and it was to become an even bigger story because of the man in the photograph.

This was not the Holmes photograph, though it had appeared again that year, once again providing visual proof of the ancient myth that had been relegated to the realm of the non-existent. Elliot had written to the *Listener* explaining the background to Lieutenant Holmes's confession, but he had made no reference whatsoever to the man in this more recent photograph. His letter, which ended with a repetition of the statement that the rope trick had never been performed and never would be, was, of course, immediately followed by an account from someone who had seen it performed, this time on the banks of the Ganges. There then followed a short letter on the causes of war, reminding Christian Englishmen that 'they cannot put their faith in armaments, but must use the methods of peace which Christ advocated'.[23] Yet the sides could not be reconciled, and the big debate continued to grow as Elliot persisted in denying the existence of a trick witnessed by the unknown and the unimportant, and photographed recently being performed by the unidentified. Who was this Indian man in the photograph who had supposedly performed the rope trick?

The newspaper described him as Karachi. His real name, however, was Arthur, and he was from Plymouth. Arthur Derby was the latest in a long line of fake fakirs who sought to profit from the mysterious image of the East. He had performed under a previous stage name, The Phantom, but had traded that in for the robes and dark make-up that Colonel Stodare had felt so unnecessary seven decades earlier. He was of average height, slimly built, with a rugged face and an unknown complexion. He had been taught the rope trick by a Gurkha soldier during the Great War, or so he claimed, although this was not true. He had accepted the Magic Circle challenge but received no reply, or so he claimed, but this was also untrue. He could perform the rope trick for any number of people as often as necessary, or so he claimed, and the truth of this was about to be tested. As the claims of the mysterious Karachi were discussed, some wondered whether they might be genuine, while others wondered why he had received no reply from the Magic Circle.

And there was academic interest as well. An anthropologist from King's College, Cambridge, questioned whether the man who had supposedly taught Karachi was really a Gurkha. 'I have been studying the social life of the Nepalese for some years now,' he informed the unknown and unimportant, '[but] never have I found one to have the slightest knowledge of conjuring.' Years of scholarly research had taught him, in fact, that 'the Gurkha is a completely unsophisticated peasant, and generally speaking clumsy with his hands', and his considered opinion was that the man was most likely from Darjeeling. With interest being shown by such intellectuals as well as the general public, Elliot decided to call the bluff of Karachi. In true fighting talk, the Lieutenant Colonel publicly declared he had received no challenge, but 'if we receive one we will gladly take it up'. Below Elliot's bold declaration was a letter from a gentleman critical of the use of armed force, maintaining that 'war can be prevented'.[24]

On 30 January 1935, the headline read, 'Karachi Challenges Magic Circle', and his challenge was this: he offered to perform the rope trick 'as nearly as possible under natural Indian conditions'. A rope would rise into the air, and a boy would climb to the top, in open ground, with rope that could be examined, and before an audience at least fifteen yards from him. He would, for reasons not stipulated, require forty-eight hours' access to the place of performance, with nobody spying on him. 'These are fair conditions,' he stated, 'and if the Magic Circle is really seeking enlightenment, they will accept my challenge, and this much-disputed tradition will become a reality.' The public was 'waiting with interest to see whether the Magic Circle is ready to stand to its guns and accept the challenge thrown down to it by Karachi', impatient to see 'the truth being finally exposed'. Even the *Magic Circular* noted that Karachi had 'accepted the challenge of the Occult Committee . . . his letter is intriguing and it will be interesting to know what action the Committee will take.'[25]

The Committee, however, did not take action. Elliot simply pointed out what to him was self-evident: that this was not the Indian rope trick. Referring to the original Magic Circle challenge, he repeated that 'the rope must be thrown into the air and defy the force of gravity, while someone climbs up it and disappears'. Karachi was offering no such performance, no *actual* defiance of gravity, and no disappearance of the boy.

'He does a rope trick,' Elliot admitted, but it was not the Indian rope trick, and 'does not interest us in the least'. 'Our object has been to kill off a ridiculous superstition that a miraculous Indian rope trick has been performed,' he explained. 'What we are out against is the humbug that in the rope trick there is anything supernatural,' he persisted, 'and so long as [conjurors] do not claim anything supernormal in their performances we have no quarrel with them.'[26]

All of this was true and eminently sensible, but Elliot should have known by now that truth and commonsense were not sufficient. To those who took a less than scholarly interest in the legend, this simply looked like a retreat. Elliot's attitude looked 'like hair-splitting of a not too creditable kind', said one reader; 'the truth appears to be that Karachi has put a spoke into the Magic Circle'. The Committee was accused of getting itself 'into a false position of first offering 500 guineas for the performance of a feat which it alleges is impossible, and then running away from anyone who offers to demonstrate that it is possible'. 'Very many readers', said another, 'must share my amazement and disappointment at the ignominious climb-down of the Magic Circle in its refusal to accept Karachi's very reasonable challenge.' Meanwhile, some went into tedious debates about the meaning of 'trick', others into the meaning of 'defiance of gravity', and Harold T. Wilkins reappeared to ask with characteristic scepticism, 'Is Karachi really a native of India?'[27]

But the crux of the matter was whether Karachi's performance could be called the Indian rope trick, and that was a matter to be determined by an appropriate witness. Enter Harry Price, member of the Magic Circle, and Director of the National Laboratory for Psychical Science. He had been present at the recent Magic Circle debate as a witness for the prosecution, declaring that in his enormous collection of books on magic and the paranormal, there was not a single piece of evidence in support of the rope trick. Now he arranged for Karachi to perform the rope trick in the presence of academics, scientists, and representatives of the BBC. The result, however, was less than perfect. Hoping to perform 'as nearly as possible under natural Indian conditions', Karachi chose a field north of London in 'a cold drizzle, which turned to snow'. With 'the elements raging', Karachi allowed the rope to be examined, a rope which was 'very loosely woven'. He then placed it somewhat suspiciously under a cloth, and 'an end appeared and crept upwards with a jerky motion. It was noticed that the rope was now very *tightly* woven and very rigid.' On a piece of ground that Karachi had required one week to prepare, this substituted rigid rope rose to seven or eight feet, at which point 'Karachi commanded his son to climb up it – which he did.' Later, Price explained, 'Karachi was about to tell me exactly how it was done. But I stopped him. No one needed telling how the trick was done.'[28]

Karachi (aka Arthur) and his son, posing in native costume somewhere in deepest Hertfordshire. To see what happened next, lift up this page now.

Karachi's performance was filmed at the time by the British Film Institute, and a single viewing is enough to convince anyone that it is hardly the stuff of legends. When considered by the BBC, an advisor stated that Karachi 'could not even deceive the simple onlooker who is making every allowance', and concluded, 'I do not consider that we could possibly make [this] the subject for an Outside Broadcast. The unfortunate Karachi has a good idea, but is a very poor showman [and] his props and his performance are lamentable.'[29] It was, therefore, somewhat disingenuous of Harry Price to declare with some enthusiasm, 'I have seen the Indian Rope Trick.'[30] No doubt he gained the publicity he sought, but the result was that the public were soon teasing the Magic Circle that 'Harry Price has now seen the most famous trick that has never been performed.'[31] The debate continued without further progress, and while many complained of the Occult Committee's position, the Committee refused to pay Karachi the reward he so optimistically sought. Elliot's predecessor, John Nevil Maskelyne, could at least rest in peace, safe in the knowledge that the Committee he had set up just before his death had not had to spend a penny.

One can only wonder what John E. Wilkie thought of all this, or how much he even knew of it. Since he had written the article that had inadvertently launched the legend, he had been rather busy. He had worked as a special crime reporter with

To see the boy magically returned to the ground, go back to the previous page. Repeat these actions until the novelty has worn off. If only the live performance had looked this good.

the *Tribune* in a Chicago increasingly plagued by organised crime, and he had been city editor when, in 1898, he had received a telegram from the Secretary of the Treasury to attend a meeting. At that meeting, he had been offered a job so unexpected that, in his own words, he 'nearly fell out of his chair'. 'I should like to take you to Washington,' the Secretary had told him, 'and make you Chief of the Secret Service.'[32] Wilkie's experience of special criminal investigation, his personal contacts, and his reputation for being a man 'of perfect honesty', had prompted his recommendation to the post, and he had 'accepted the surprising offer after a week of deliberation'.[33] With that, Wilkie had entered a whole new world of fraud, deceit and propaganda.

The Service had been set up by Lincoln at the end of the Civil War primarily to investigate counterfeiting. By 1898, however, a $100m counterfeiting ring had forced a recall of an entire issue of currency, and Wilkie's first job had been to smash this ring, which he had done through the ingenious use of disinformation.[34] Shortly afterwards, with the outbreak of the Spanish-American war, he had immediately requested extra funds in order to establish a counterespionage force. This force had carried out surveillance of Spanish spies based in Montreal and led by a Spanish aristocrat called Carranza. It soon led to the arrest of a man who, according to Carranza, was 'one of their two best spies'. The man was later found dead in his cell, allegedly having hanged himself, though according to Carranza, 'they did it for him'. Continued surveillance had finally led to the expulsion of Carranza himself, thanks to the discovery of an incriminating letter. Wilkie later called the letter 'one of the sensations of the war', as a result of which the 'Spanish spy-system received its death-blow'. The following year, however, stories had appeared claiming that Wilkie had forged the letter.[35]

Wilkie's understanding of fraud was matched by propaganda skills learned as a journalist. He exploited the press more than his predecessors had done, controlling their access to information, and ensuring that his agents' activities were hailed as a public victory. He gained something of a 'reputation as a Sherlock Holmes', and had been sent requests to solve cases of bank robbery, murder and kidnapping.[36] Yet his claims smacked of hyperbole and sensationalism at a time when '[l]urid headlines distorted the truth as a matter of routine'.[37] And if Wilkie had a tendency to be creative when telling a story about the solving of a mystery, he also seems to have been able to recognise a hoax when he heard it. In 1909, rumours had emerged of a conspiracy to assassinate US President Taft and Mexican President Diaz. Four decades after Lincoln had established the Secret Service, the protection of the President was now its responsibility, following the assassination of President McKinley in 1903. The Taft–Diaz conspiracy had turned out to be a myth, but while some in the security forces seem to have taken it extremely seriously, a

John E. Wilkie in his Secret Service office, checking out the usual suspects. One suspects the master of deception is aware his own picture is being taken.

COPYRIGHT BY WALDON FAWCETT.

man of Wilkie's experience was not to be fooled. '[T]he case was on the face of it so absurd that it should never have been given serious attention,' it was later pointed out, yet 'Wilkie and his men stood alone in their insistence that the affair was a hoax.'[38]

Wilkie had left the Secret Service in 1912, and spent the remainder of his life in his home town as a senior official of Chicago Street Railway Lines and of the Chicago Railway Company. There he could read in his old newspaper of the continued rise of organised crime in the city, born in response to his old editor's mayoral policies, investigated by himself, and now peaking under the ruthless tactics of Alphonse Capone. In his study was 'a collection of criminal relics – counterfeiting paraphernalia, bogus money, pistols, sinister knives . . . Several of them had been seized in desperate hand-to-hand struggles.'[39] And he could reminisce about the adventures had by him and his agents. In characteristic sensationalist language, he told the story of Marco Santoro, alias the Lone Wolf, the 'most infamous and heartless knife thrower in Italy', who had killed several of his countrymen before coming to New York to engage in counterfeiting. Santoro was informed on by his own wife, Maria, whom he had stabbed and left for dead in London, while she was carrying his child. He had escaped the clutches of Scotland Yard and fled to New York with an unscrupulous French blonde. Yet Wilkie's men had finally cornered him in

Manhattan, and before he could draw and throw his notorious knife, one of the agents shot him dead.[40]

On 14 December 1934, John E. Wilkie died in more peaceful circumstances, of 'a heart ailment'. Newspaper obituaries recounted many of his 'spectacular exploits'. His son recalled how even he had been excluded from his father's business secrets, a fact he had realised when they travelled together to Europe and Wilkie 'vanished for nearly a month and a half'.[41] Political historians would remember Wilkie for, among other things, paying his men without Congressional authorisation, for being accused of secretly investigating members of cabinet and Congress, and for providing Roosevelt with special agents in order to set up the Bureau of Investigation, later known as the FBI. He would be remembered by others for having shaped the modern Secret Service, for his detective abilities, his deceptive methods, and his aptitude for story-telling and disinformation. Yet he would not be remembered for his most famous story and most successful piece of disinformation.

That same year, just months before Wilkie died, the BBC broadcast a radio programme from London about a story 'which everybody's heard of' – the Indian rope trick. It had been suggested that the story could 'be traced back to one which appeared in an American newspaper [around 1890] . . . and which had simply been invented, by a journalist'. 'Well,' the BBC declared of this suggestion, 'it's absolutely absurd.' If John E. Wilkie had been listening, he would not have heard his name mentioned. Indeed, had he lived for the remainder of the century, he would not have had to answer any questions about his surreptitious role in the rise of one of the world's most famous mysteries. At the end of a remarkable life of secrets, his most unusual secret was safe.

So the man who had launched the legend of the Indian rope trick was dead, but the legend itself lived on, and grew not only older but larger. Witnesses would continue to appear claiming they had seen the trick with their own eyes. Meanwhile, with the father of the legend now not only gone but forgotten, historians would go in search of its origins and discover an ancient tradition concerning a considerably more gruesome feat. Under pressure to explain this inexplicable and bloody miracle, conjurors, scientists and some extraordinary individuals would claim they knew how it could be performed. Yet questions would continue to surround the legend of the rope trick. Why did Wilkie never receive any recognition? How could an impossible feat be made possible? And what did the witnesses really see?

PART III

A LEGEND UNRAVELLED

8

The Search for the Origins of the Legend

By the end of 1934, public interest in the rope trick was greater than it had ever been. Elliot had done his best to kill off the legend, but the newspapers recognised a good story when they saw one, and Elliot could not compete with the endless articles and letters expressing a less than sceptical position. Even the BBC had taken an interest in the Karachi challenge, though they had not regarded it as good television. Instead, it was featured on a popular radio programme. 'Good evening, everybody,' the announcer began, 'I want to talk to you about the famous Indian rope-trick.' He hoped to put to rest 'various widespread notions about the trick, which are mostly wrong'. One of these wrong notions was the opinion that the trick could be traced back to an American newspaper hoax half a century earlier, a notion which, as we have seen, he declared to be 'absolutely absurd'.[1] And this statement was made on expert authority. For magic historians had gone in search of the roots of the rope trick legend, and had found evidence that it had been around before 1890. Some claimed that in 1875 a huge reward had been offered throughout India for a single performance. Others pointed out that it had been reported by travellers as far back as the fourteenth century. And one man concluded that there was clearly a popular belief in the rope trick at least 3500 years ago. They were not entirely wrong, but they were certainly not entirely right, and their conclusions led to a history in which the Indian rope trick was not Indian and did not use a rope, and which completely ignored John E. Wilkie. How this happened is a curious lesson in the construction of history, and it begins with a story about a prince.

In 1875, Albert Edward, the Prince of Wales, had visited India, and it had not been for a holiday. This had been a major diplomatic expedition, the cost of which had been estimated at sixty thousand pounds, the return inestimable. India had recently become officially British. In the aftermath of the 1857 Uprising, played down by colonial historians as a 'Mutiny' of sepoys, the Crown had taken over administrative duties from the East India Company, and Victoria was now to be pronounced Empress of India. The Prince of Wales's mission had been to raise the profile of the monarchy among its new subjects, to provide 'an outward and visible sign of the personal existence of the Power which had control of their destinies'.[2] This had required several months of travel around the subcontinent, though His Royal Highness had been made as comfortable as possible. Indeed, the royal diarist described all manner of entertainments laid on for the Prince, and naturally this had included those renowned Indian jugglers, who had gone out of their way to impress the heir to the throne. In Madras, one juggler 'took live scorpions out of his mouth; spat out stones as large as plums and swallowed them; evolved from internal depths large and small nails and string, till there was a pile of his products before the Prince'. Looking up from this impressive pile, the Prince had savoured 'a strong-limbed comely young woman' who had stretched her legs behind her head, and bent 'backwards till she could put her hands on the ground'. Whatever had crossed His royal mind had then been abruptly interrupted by a man who had thrown a coconut in the air and 'as it fell, met it with the top of his naked skull'.[3] The jugglers had also performed their greatest and most famous feats, including the basket trick, the mango trick, and snake charming. But there had been no mention of the Indian rope trick since, in 1875, nobody had heard of it.

Half a century later, however, everyone had heard of it, and some went in search of its roots. Carl Hertz, who had searched in India for the secret to the trick, and who claimed to have found it, also claimed the trick had been famous for at least half a century. 'When the late King Edward VII, then

Prince of Wales, went to India in 1876,' Hertz informed his readers, 'that country was, at his special request, scoured to find someone who could perform the trick.'[4] Another magic historian agreed, informing his readers that 'in 1875, Lord Northbrook, the Viceroy, had advertised by proclamation throughout all India, offering 10,000 pounds sterling as a reward to any wonder-worker who could do this very trick'.[5] If this were true, of course, it is not surprising that nobody gave Wilkie any credit for having launched the legend. But if this were true, it would not be difficult to check. After all, with such a reward being offered for a performance of the trick – no less than a sixth of the total cost of the Prince's tour of India – one can imagine the huge publicity that would have been generated, the endless comments that would have been made. One can imagine all manner of things that would have been written, perhaps, but one cannot actually find anything.

The Times, for example, as it gave a detailed breakdown of the Prince's expenses to its readership of taxpayers, did not mention the reward. The diarist of the Prince's tour, who described the various feats of Indian juggling actually seen by the Prince, did not mention it either. Lord Northbrook, according to a book about his short time as Viceroy, did not say a word about this enormous reward he is supposed to have offered.[6] In fact, none of them referred to the Indian rope trick at all, and neither did contemporary writers on Indian magic.[7] Louis Jacolliot's *Occult Science in India* was first published in English in 1884, and sought to 'pay particular attention to the phenomena which the fakirs produce', yet it made no mention of the Indian rope trick.[8] Indeed, every book in which you might expect to find a mention of the legendary trick is silent. And it is not only books, for Victorian newspapers often discussed Indian juggling, and none of them mentioned the Indian rope trick before 1890. Just two years before Wilkie's story appeared, the *Graphic* published an illustrated story about 'Magic in India', referred to the mango trick, the basket trick, and snake charming, but made no reference to any rope trick.[9] Surely they would have mentioned a trick so famous that the whole of India had been scoured for it at the special request of the Prince of Wales, so sought-after that the Viceroy himself had offered ten thousand pounds for a single performance?

But they did not mention it, because they had never heard of it. There was no evidence that any reward had been offered in 1875. It seems, in fact, that those who thought there had been one simply got mixed up with a later Prince of Wales and a different reward.[10] A simple error, perhaps, but one that was taken as fact for the rest of the twentieth century.[11] And if the Indian rope trick was already famous in 1875 then its roots clearly had to be older, and so even those who later knew of Wilkie's story could not have thought it was the source of the legend's rise to fame. Meanwhile, historians looked further and further back in search of the origins of the legend, and found many Indian rope tricks that were indeed older, even if they were not about ropes in India.

There were many contenders for the original Indian rope trick. The most obvious was Jahangir's chain trick, which had been described by the Moghul Emperor in the seventeenth century. It had been about a chain, of course, which had risen into the air, after which several animals had climbed up the chain and disappeared, but at least it was from India. Those who sought the origins of the legend, however, were interested in the age of the story rather than its location. What mattered to them was how old the story was, rather than whether it came from India. And so they found earlier rope tricks, one from seventeenth-century China, and another from sixteenth-century Germany, and other rope tricks were found in Indonesia and Ireland. The oldest story they found, however, was the leather thong trick that had caused Ibn Battuta to faint in fourteenth-century China. As far as S. W. Clarke, editor of the *Magic Circular*, was concerned, the rope trick 'was first described by the Arab traveller, Ibn Battuta, who said that he saw it in China'.[12] This being the earliest known eye-witness account, the Chinese thong trick came to be seen as the original Indian rope trick, and Elliot declared that, 'since the earliest records of it go back, not to Hindustan, but to China', the Indian rope trick 'is not Indian'.[13]

This Chinese claim to the most famous of Indian legends did not go unchallenged, however, and soon there was a debate in India that sought to reclaim its Indian roots. When a letter to the *Times of India* asked, 'Did Ibn Battuta institute one of the greatest hoaxes in history?', the reply had nothing to do with Wilkie.[14] Instead, a correspondent claimed that eye-witnesses to the trick could be found in ancient Indian Sutras. It was claimed that Sutra 1-1-17 of the Vedanta Sutras spoke of 'the illusory juggler who climbs up the rope and disappears'.[15] But an Indian correspondent soon pointed out that this was a mistranslation of the original Sanskrit, and that it should read simply 'the magician who with sword and shield climbs up the rope'.[16] There was no mention of a rope rising in the air, or of the magician disappearing, merely of a rope being climbed, not in itself anything remarkable. He also pointed out, for the record, that the reference was made not in the original Sutras, but in a much later commentary by Sankara, the eighth-century philosopher. Nevertheless, this reference continued to be presented as evidence of the ancient Indian roots of the rope trick. H. L. Varma, Minister of Surguja State, published a book in 1942 that maintained 'that the trick is of Indian origin . . . and although it may have been performed in China also, it is of hoary antiquity so far as India is concerned'. Confusing the eighth-century commentary with the original Sutra, he claimed that while this 'does not prove that Vyas the author of the Sutra himself saw the trick 3500 years ago, it certainly does establish that a popular belief about the trick did exist then as it does now'.[17]

By now, the rope trick was being seen in truly mythical terms, and the debate was soon joined by those with expertise in mythology. They pointed out that Sankara had spoken of a rope trick elsewhere. In a different commentary, this time on the Mandukya Upanishad, Sankara had written of 'a juggler [who] throws the end of a thread up in the sky, and climbing by the help of the thread disappears . . . His body begins to fall to the ground in pieces which unite anon into the self-same juggler.'[18] Surely this was a contender for the original Indian rope trick? Yet the search continued and even older sources were found. In the Jatakas, tales of the previous lives of the Buddha that had been compiled no later than the fifth century BC, there was a tale of a juggler who:

> threw up a ball of string, and made it catch on a branch of [a] tree, and then up he climbed . . . [Slaves] chopt him up limb-meal and threw down the bits. The other jugglers joined the pieces together, and poured water upon them. The man donned upper and under garments of flowers, and rose up and began dancing again.[19]

It seemed that the Indian rope trick was indeed 'of hoary antiquity so far as India was concerned'. But as the debate grew in the twentieth century, it became increasingly apparent that the legend was also of hoary antiquity so far as many other countries were concerned. Mircea Eliade, the highly respected scholar of religion, wrote about the ancient roots of the rope trick in several books. He pointed out that the Australian Wiradjuri tribe spoke of shamans that climbed cords to reach the heavens, of a Siberian shaman who 'relates how he mounts to the sky by the help of a rope', of a Mara medicine man's powers to climb 'by means of a rope, invisible to ordinary mortals, into the sky, where he can hold converse with the star people'. He explained that the Maori hero 'Tawhaki goes up into the sky by climbing a vine and, later, succeeds in returning to earth . . . According to other variants the hero reaches the sky by climbing a coconut palm, or by a rope, a spider web, or a kite. In the Hawaiian Islands, he is said to climb the rainbow.' The sheer diversity of these stories from every corner of the world was, for Eliade, evidence of a 'more general belief regarding the medicine man's ability to reach the sky by means of a rope, a scarf, or simply by flying or climbing a spiral staircase'.[20] And yet, when Eliade wrote about 'the rope trick', his first example was of a poem about the Buddha, 'who raised himself in the air and cut his body into pieces, which he dropped to the ground and then joined together again beneath the astonished eyes of the spectators'.[21] From all of the rope tricks in all of the world, he had chosen one from India after all, but one that did not have a rope of any

PUNCH, *or The London Charivari* August 15, 1934

PROBABLE INVENTION OF THE INDIAN ROPE TRICK.

An early performance of the rope trick attracts a curious audience.

description. Anyone seeking the origins of the legend was being offered a growing list of contenders, and the list seemed to be wide open to both non-Indian and ropeless candidates. Writing a history of the Indian rope trick was becoming increasingly difficult, but at least one thing was clear: the idea that it was launched in Chicago in 1890 was absurd. Wasn't it?

As the legend continued to grow in the middle of the twentieth century, the debate about its origins was only making the origins seem all the more mysterious. But much of the confusion arose from disagreement about what the Indian rope trick was, and why it mattered. Like those who had searched in India for the secret to the rope trick and found many secrets, those who sought the origin of the legend had found different origins because they were looking in different places for different reasons. They were looking for a rope trick, but not necessarily an Indian one. They were magicians in search of a trick, or psychical researchers curious about a possible psychic phenomenon, or scholars of religion writing about a mythical theme. For some it was the mystery that mattered. Was the rope trick real? How was it done? For others it was its ubiquity, which demonstrated the mythical significance of the story. But none of them was particularly concerned with its location, and so they went looking far and wide, and found rope tricks in many times and places.

But the location was important, for it was not the Chinese rope trick that became the greatest legend of the East, it was not Chinese jugglers whose reputation supported the legend – nobody went to search for the trick in China. It was a story about a trick with a rope in India that captured the popular imagination and became the world's most famous illusion, and that fame matters too. Without it, people would not have searched throughout India or offered large rewards in the hope of finding the trick, there would not have been an enthusiastic public debate about whether it was real, and magicians and scholars would not have been discussing its origins in the first place. Without that fame, it would not have become the greatest legend of the East, and you would not be reading this book. That fame is what matters to the historian, what makes it history rather than an unrecorded part of the past. That is why the question of the origins of the legend is best directed to when the Indian rope trick rose to fame, for until it had entered the popular imagination, the legend had not yet been born.

Throughout the twentieth century, there were various theories about when that had happened. But since nobody questioned the claim concerning the Prince of Wales, it was assumed that it had happened before 1875.[22] Some suggested the legend had been invented by the British following the 1857 Uprising in order to attract more army recruits to India.[23] A journalist, on the other hand, claimed it had been a subject of public debate '[s]ince Europeans first settled in India'.[24] And there were, of course, the various stories that seemed to place the Indian rope trick in the popular imagination of our distant ancestors.[25] But whatever else our ancestors might have imagined, they were not imagining an Indian rope trick until the nineteenth century, and at first they were thinking of something entirely different.

In the 1860s, when a conjuror boasted on his playbill that he 'Nightly accomplishes the Wonderful Indian Rope Trick to the Delight of Crowded and Fashionable Audiences', he was promising a quite different rope trick.[26] This was the rope escape that had been performed by Indian jugglers, and that had been adapted by the Davenport brothers as an apparent display of spirit manifestations. In 1880, when *The Great Wizard's Handbook* was sold to the public on the basis that it contained the secret to 'the rope trick', that is what was meant.[27] There was no confusion among the public at that time because they had no knowledge of any other Indian rope trick.[28]

They might, of course, have heard of Ibn Battuta's Chinese thong trick, or Jahangir's chain trick. Both of them had been translated into English in the nineteenth century, both had appeared in Henry Yule's book on Marco Polo in 1873, and both had been described in 1877 by Madame Blavatsky as examples of what she called the 'Indian tape-climbing trick'. But they were not themselves Indian rope tricks, neither literally nor in the popular imagination. Blavatsky may have referred to them as Indian, but her writings were hardly well known, and so far as the thong and chain tricks were known, both had been, and continued to be, associated with China.[29] Even John Nevil Maskelyne, who publicly criticised Madame Blavatsky, and was no friend of Indian jugglers, thought that Jahangir's chain trick had taken place in China, and had been performed by Chinese jugglers.[30]

And what about Sankara's commentary on the Mandukya Upanishad? He had spoken of a trick that was both Indian and about a rope, and had done so back in the eighth century. But it had been written in Sanskrit, a language virtually unknown in the West until the nineteenth century, and not published in English until 1894. Before then, only those who read Sanskrit would have been aware of it, and then only if they had noticed it.[31] It was, after all, only one sentence. Sankara used it once as a metaphor for maya, the Hindu concept of the world as an illusion. And even if you had asked a Sanskrit scholar about the rope trick that Sankara used as a metaphor for maya, he would have imagined something quite different. For Sankara repeatedly used another rope illusion as a metaphor for maya, what became known as the rope–snake metaphor – where a man sees a snake, then realises it is only a piece of rope – and which has been written about extensively since.[32] As far as Sankara or anyone who read his commentary was concerned, this was the rope trick that mattered.[33]

Despite all the earlier stories and references, it was not until after Wilkie's story that a trick with a boy and a rope came to be popularly associated with India. And while the story spread rapidly in the West, it was still relatively unknown in India a generation after Wilkie's article. Horace Goldin toured India during the Great War, and had been surprised that Indian magicians 'knew nothing of such a trick. I approached learned men who had lived many years in the East, and they told me the same story; they knew nothing of such a trick.'[34] In 1921, an Indian magician who had 'spent the better part of his life in Magic Research' had never heard of it, though his 'colleagues and friends in the profession are scattered throughout the country and they represent all branches of magic'.[35] An American magician who toured India around the same time 'was surprised to learn that not one of the three thousand fakirs, conjurers and magicians had ever heard of it'.[36] But by the 1930s, the Indian press was talking about the legend and its origins, and it was not long before there were claims that it was of hoary antiquity so far as India was concerned.

As stories from all over the world were identified as earlier Indian rope tricks, the origins of the legend were assumed to be lost in the distant past, and the man who started its rise to fame was ignored. But there was another consequence of the search for the origins, for as the legend grew in fame, it also grew in form. For the most part, during the decades following

1890, it had remained a relatively simple affair: a rope was thrown into the air, a boy climbed up it and disappeared. This, according to John Nevil Maskelyne in 1908, was the 'commonly accepted version'.[37] By 1934, the variety of rope tricks that had appeared led Elliot to stress the need for:

> a clear understanding of what we mean by the Indian rope trick. A fakir . . . throws a rope into the air where it remains suspended, defying the law of gravity. A boy climbs up and disappears. The rope falls down and the boy reappears, none the worse for his experience. When people say that they have seen the Indian rope trick, that is what the public understand by their claim.[38]

That was also the version most witnesses had reported, and it is what the Magic Circle challenge of 1934 demanded.

But as Ibn Battuta's thong trick came to be seen as the classic version, and with similar tales emerging all the time, the Indian rope trick increasingly came to be described in more gruesome terms. It was not long before Maskelyne's son, Jasper, publicly noted that 'the real Indian rope-trick is more than this'. After the boy disappears, the magician follows with a knife, 'whereupon pieces of the boy's body fall to the ground'.[39] The dismemberment came to be seen as a necessary part of the rope trick, and for some, such as Eliade, it was more important than the rope itself.[40] At times, this bloody version of the rope trick was presented to the public in graphic detail. In 1938, *Today* newspaper published a fully illustrated story about a sadhu (i.e., fakir) who had hypnotised a crowd into seeing the whole gory spectacle. The performance had been filmed, and stills were accompanied by a running commentary in the present tense:

> They have seen the rope rise into the air and the boy has climbed it. The drama is about to begin . . . the sadhu again turns his hypnotic eyes upon the crowd . . . [and] the boy gradually fades . . . into thin air. Horror seizes the watchers as the sadhu draws his sword. Carrying it in his mouth . . . he climbs too and disappears. . . . The crowd watches the trick in wonder. Spectators scream as they gaze fascinated at the rope, when suddenly the trunk and limbs of the boy fall from the sky and lie bleeding upon the ground . . . It looks as though the unfortunate boy has been murdered.[41]

The boy, of course, was just fine, since the whole thing had never really happened. But if the readers were convinced by such proof of the powers of mass hypnosis, they were soon to be informed how this non-event had been filmed. It was, in fact, a 'filmic interpretation' using actors, to show 'exactly what the spectator sees'. The headline read, 'First Genuine Photographs of the Indian Rope Trick', but they were not genuine photographs, and since it was two decades since

Lieutenant Holmes had faked his own genuine photograph, they were not the first either. Nevertheless, as far as readers were concerned, this horrific spectacle was the Indian rope trick.

The pre-war sensationalist press seems to have enjoyed such startling images. In that same year of 1938, when journalists might have concerned themselves with more pressing matters, the front page of the *Sunday Graphic* asked, 'Is this the most amazing picture ever taken?' Its answer, however, had nothing to do with the approaching war, or the rope trick. The caption to this truly amazing picture was 'LION ATTACKS GIRL', and it was a picture of a girl supposedly being attacked by a lion. The girl, arms raised and mouth open in an attempt to look terrified, does not. There is a man on the right looking on and yelling, apparently at the lion to stop, but more likely at the girl to look more convincing. The lion has its back to camera. Unable to compete with the most amazing picture ever taken, a story entitled 'Indian Rope Trick Filmed by British Army' was relegated to the inside pages, though it did receive more space, included more pictures, and involved a terrifying array of fonts. Those who had survived the horror of the front page could read of how Captain Durtnell of the Royal West Kent Regiment had filmed the trick near the Bhurtpore Barracks in India. It was, of course, a hoax, and was admitted to be so in the smallest font available to the moody typesetter. But if the most amazing picture ever taken is any

SPRING FASHION SECRETS IN PICTURES

SUNDAY GRAPHIC
and SUNDAY NEWS

No. 1,191.   SUNDAY, JANUARY 30, 1938.   TWOPENCE.

Is This The Most Amazing Picture Ever Taken?

LION ATTACKS GIRL

THIS amazing and exclusive picture reached the "Sunday Graphic" last night. Ione Reed, the wild animal girl, was rehearsing a lion when it suddenly turned to attack her.

She owes her life to the trainer, who is seen hurrying to her assistance. The incident took place at the Zoo in Los Angeles.

Even the rope trick could not compete with the most amazing picture ever taken. It is believed the girl survived to enjoy a successful career in horror movies. The lion was returned to its display cabinet.

reflection of their critical abilities, readers of the *Sunday Graphic* are unlikely to have noticed.

By now, of course, John E. Wilkie was dead, but the legend he had launched with a hoax was healthy, regenerated by further hoaxes. It had grown steadily for half a century, and was now considered to be many centuries old. But as it had grown old it had grown larger and uglier, and this bloodier rope trick was to dominate the legend. Wilkie's more innocent version, it was recently declared, 'is not the legendary Indian rope trick', for what made the legend so sensational was the blood and body parts of the boy.[42] Perhaps this was true – it was certainly much more exciting stuff – but surely nobody would believe it was real. Perhaps the public might be deceived by the hoaxes, but magicians would surely know better. Yet history is a powerful discourse, and who can doubt the evidence of so many centuries? Before long, magicians were coming up with bizarre explanations for how the whole gory episode could actually be performed.

9

How to Perform the Impossible

In the aftermath of the great debate of 1934, the rope trick was firmly established as 'the world's most famous illusion', and had 'invited greater discussion and provoked more mystery than any other piece of magic in the world'.[1] This would remain the case throughout the century, for much of this discussion and mystery concerned whether it actually existed and, if it did, how it could be done. The existence of the rope trick was now seemingly demonstrated by an ancient tradition, and eye-witnesses since the fourteenth century, not to mention more recent genuine photographs. 'So it seems quite certain', one commentator would announce, 'that the feat has been accomplished. It remains for us to examine the methods.'[2] And so the secret of the world's most famous illusion came under scrutiny. There had, of course, been a tradition in the West of explaining how the feats of Indian juggling were done, but those feats had been easier to find. Conversely, long searches and large rewards had failed to secure a performance of the rope trick, so some imaginative thinking was going to be necessary. After all, even the eye-witnesses who occasionally declared they had seen the trick were not reporting the gruesome, but now official, legendary version of the trick. Nevertheless, the public were in need of an explanation, and various authorities felt under pressure to provide one. And so they took their turns in trying to explain what was not only inexplicable but also unnecessary.

Needless to say, Western conjurors had been quick to respond to the challenge. As soon as stories of the rope trick had appeared, they had at first dismissed them as nonsense, but then recognised the potential profitability of performing the trick. There had been several stage versions already by most of the great conjurors of the day. But these performances had exploited the advantages of the stage environment, and what made the rope trick so impressive was that it was supposedly being performed in the open air. This had seemed to rule out normal conjuring methods, and so some had felt there must be other forces at work. According to the *Occult Review*, early missionaries in India:

at a loss to account for it, very promptly attributed it to the devil, and this ingenious explanation is still persisted in by the missionaries of the present, who assert that it is a sin even to witness these performances, and who anathematise the Sadhus as agents of Satan.[3]

Less diabolical explanations had also been suggested by minds that enjoyed the creative freedom of an imagination unrestricted by any practical knowledge of conjuring. *Edwards Monthly* had noted back in 1909 that the trick 'has not to our knowledge been fully explained' and so remained 'to the average mind, a mystery'. In the opinion of the author, however, the secret was 'simpler than the spectator imagines', and he had explained all. '[T]he fakir and his assistants make plenty of noise singing and chanting and swinging their arms,' he had informed the average-minded, then the rope is set on fire and 'swung a few times about the fakir's head, after which he suddenly thrusts the burning end into his mouth'. Under cover of this natural misdirection, and 'a cloud of heavy smoke, blue in colour . . . a slender line is dropped from a nearby house' and attached to the other end of the rope. As the rope is thrown in the air, this line is pulled in and 'it is easily seen why the rope hangs in the air. Then the fakir starts a lot of wailing and beating of his breast.' Amid much noise, and a great deal of smoke, a second heavy rope is lowered and attached with a metal catch to the first rope, which is hauled up, along with the wailing fakir, by his assistants on top of the nearby roof.[4]

Whether or not anybody thought this simple, some seem to have been convinced that this was the true secret. Years later, it had reappeared in a popular science magazine, no doubt keen to establish scientific authority in matters of the unexplained. This time, however, the explanation had been presented as the result of 'a painstaking study' recently carried out in Bombay 'by a scientist'. As part of this rigorous experiment, the scientist had sneaked into a house 'without being seen by the natives. He had found a little window which gave him a view of the courtyard and the tops of the surrounding houses.' From there, our intrepid experimenter had watched the rope being set on fire, swung around the fakir's head, and plunged into his mouth. Trained in detached observation, however, he had spotted the various ropes and lines being tied together, and the assistants on top of the roof hauling the fakir upwards. All of this had been cunningly concealed, observed the scientific expert, by 'a little bundle of some smoking, smouldering substance'. This, the journal had claimed, was 'the only explanation ever made of the famous rope-climbing trick', and the secret having been once again 'revealed at last', science had gone on to explain how the mango trick was performed using mass hypnosis.[5]

With amateur guesswork like this, conjurors had naturally felt under pressure to provide more practical solutions, and none more so than John Nevil Maskelyne, the man who had already revealed so much about Indian juggling. He had purportedly found a gentleman who knew the secret, and had passed it on to the public in 1913. The rope, he had claimed, was 'jointed bamboos with the joints made to lock. It was covered to look like a rope, and it formed a pole about thirty feet long. A diminutive boy, not much larger than an Indian monkey, climbed to the top of the pole and was out of sight.' This was because the audience had been cleverly situated on the balcony, shielded from the sun by an awning, and if they had bent forward to see the boy, 'the sun shone in their eyes and blinded them'.[6] A version of this explanation had subsequently been heard by Major Branson, that defender of empire, who replied with characteristic open-mindedness, 'I make no comment on this explanation. It is not worthy of one.'[7]

With science and magic unable to solve the problem, the British aristocracy had felt it should clear matters up. Lord Frederic Hamilton, fourth son of the first Duke of Abercorn, a Harrow-educated former diplomat and regular at the Carlton Club, had provided his own theory in 1921. He had been told by Colonel Barnard, Chief of Police in Calcutta, that he had seen a performance of the rope trick in 'a small courtyard thick with the dense smoke arising from two braziers burning mysterious compounds'. Was this, perhaps, the previously identified 'smoking, smouldering substance'? Barnard claims he took photographs, but the developed pictures 'were simply blanks, showing details of the courtyard and nothing else'. There was, of course, nothing new about this story, and his lordship had naturally suspected hypnotic passes were involved at some point, but he had also suggested another theory relating to the mysterious substance. 'Possibly the braziers contained cunning preparations of hemp or opium unknown to European science,' opined his lordship, 'or some other brain-stealers.'[8] Such insight did not impress Elliot, who had 'no patience with all this loose talk about the mysterious drugs of the East. The people who put forward such ideas know nothing . . . these absurd propositions . . . are the hallmark of ignorance and credulity.'[9] In any case, his lordship had been speaking of a relatively simple and bloodless rope trick. A more cruel version of the trick was now demanding explanation, and if its secret was known to anyone, who better than a super-magician with a streak of cruelty?

Erik Jan Hanussen, who billed himself as the 'Mental Wizard of all Ages', had a background in blackmail and, if we are to believe him, lion-taming. Hanussen also claimed clairvoyant and telepathic powers and, in 1930s Germany, spoke of his audiences as '[m]ental weaklings, miracle-seekers, hysterics, a few truly unhappy souls . . . I am stronger than they, more courageous, more energetic, and determined . . . they are children, and I am a man.' He conducted seances for Hermann Goering, and acted as a psychic consultant to Hitler, predicting his rise to power. Had

Hitler been aware, however, that Hanussen had actually been born a 'Hebrew male', he might have been confused about such a prediction, and had his Jewish clairvoyant thrown out of the Nazi party. Needless to say, Hanussen was living dangerously, and despite having influential connections, he must have foreseen his own fate. In 1933, he was assassinated by a unit led by a senior SA man who owed him money, acting on orders from Hitler.[10] But before Hanussen met his end, he claimed he had seen the rope trick near the ruins of Babylon, and had discovered its secret.

According to Hanussen in 1930, the rope was a 'cleverly constructed apparatus, cut from the bones of sheep's (rams') vertebrae and skilfully covered with sailing cord . . . by cleverly twisting the "rope", the at first flexible material is turned into a solid stick'. This was supported from beneath the ground by helpers 'secretly concealed in a previously cleverly constructed pit'. The boy then climbed up the stick, followed by the magician, and both vanished. Apparently they had 'surrounded themselves with "clouds" by means of some "smoke"-producing preparation not known to us'. Along with the now familiar mysterious substance, 'the blinding sun in our eyes . . . created the illusion of complete disappearance', and then the dismemberment followed. Some terrible screams were heard, then 'stuffed rags which had been stained with animal blood' fell from the sky, and were placed inside a basket. The little boy meanwhile hid under the magician's robes as he descended the rope. Back on the ground, he sneaked into the basket without being seen, then jumped out of it in perfect health.[11]

In the 1930s, then, the public were faced with a growing list of theories, yet the choice remained limited. Those who declined to accept the views of a British aristocrat or a Jewish Nazi were left with the supposedly simpler explanations of the amateur scientist and the professional conjuror. Yet Karachi's dismal attempts to recreate the legendary feat in 1934 only demonstrated how difficult it was to perform the rope trick with a trick rope, and made Hanussen's method all the more unbelievable.[12] The fact was that, far from performing the dismemberment and restoration of the boy, nobody could come up with a practical method for making him vanish at the top of the rope in the open air. Conjurors continued to have problems performing the trick, and even on stage were unable to come up with an adequate representation of the larger version of the trick. In one unfortunate stage version of 1934:

> the electricians turned on the wrong lights and the audience plainly saw the thin wire . . . [then the boy] climbed up the rope with no trouble. But instead of vanishing into thin air the audience had the pleasure of seeing him leap away . . . And last – worst of all . . . before [the magician] had assembled all the arms and legs and feet and hands and head – the boy stepped out from the wings – too soon, too soon![13]

Needless to say, sceptics continued to dismiss the idea that the trick could be performed in the open air, while others continued to suggest colourful possibilities. In the midst of this confusion, one well-known American magician helpfully declared that '[t]here are thirty-five different methods of creating the illusion of the rope trick. Many of them are impossible.'[14] Hoping to obtain an expert synopsis on the current state of affairs, the *Sunday Express* announced in 1935, and in very large font, 'the secret of the Indian rope trick' by Will Goldston, founding president of the London Magicians' Club. 'Mr Goldston tells below how the trick is performed,' a smaller font claimed, but Mr Goldston did not. He explained that the theory that the rope was 'held by wire . . . was a joke', and that 'a bamboo rod, covered with rope' could at most account for a fraction of the trick. As for the full version with the boy that disappears and is dismembered, he assured readers that '[i]f it does exist, it is worked by methods completely unknown to Western magic and science'.[15]

But if the secret was unknown to Western magicians and scientists, perhaps it was time to ask Indian magicians. They had been asked before, of course, since Western conjurors had first gone looking for the trick all over India but, at that time, Indian magicians had not yet heard of it. By the 1930s, however, the rope trick was not only well known in India but was regarded there as being of Indian origin. This, then, might be a better time to ask, but there remained the problem of whom to ask, and where such a wise man might be found. The large rewards offered in newspapers had never succeeded in locating the secret, but perhaps there were reasons for that. Some suggested that holy men would not be interested in material reward, others felt that a magician might be reluctant to perform in front of a professional rival.[16] Or perhaps they had been asking in the wrong places. 'It had never occurred to their naive ethnocentric minds', it was later pointed out, 'that fakirs are not the sorts of chaps who pass a quiet afternoon at the local gentlemen's club reading the English-language newspapers.'[17] According to Will Goldston, 'the men who are said to perform the trick are poor nomadic conjurers', and as another expert helpfully pointed out, 'India's a huge place.'[18] And, as an Indian magician by the name of Professor Belzibub later declared, the rope trick could be performed by yogis and mahatmas who were masters of the power of thought, but they were 'very rarely found on account of their keeping aloof from crowded places. They generally live in mountains and dense jungles or forests.'[19] So even those who believed there was a way of performing the rope trick, and that it might be somewhere in India, realised it could be some time before the true secret would be found.

It was indeed some years later that a quite different India was to provide the next clue to the secret of the rope trick. It was an independent, but smaller India, now partially sandwiched between East and West Pakistan. It was also, under the leadership of Nehru, in the process of modernisation. Messy as this concept is, it could easily be said (indeed it was often said) that, in certain respects, India was becoming more like the modern West.[20] But for all those who held that view in the post-war West, there were many more for whom post-colonial India never lost its strange and mysterious otherness. The image of the mystic East survived the end of empire, and the legend of the Indian rope trick continued to attract those in need of a mystery that only India could provide.

Such a man was John Keel, a journalist with a keen interest in the unusual. Indeed, he would go on to write *Visitors from Space*, an 'astonishing true story' of a seven-foot-tall alien with glowing red eyes and a ten-foot wingspan. This creature, known as the Mothman, 'evoked unspeakable terrors. Like flying saucers, it delighted in chasing cars, a very unbirdlike habit, and seemed to have a penchant for scaring females who were menstruating.'[21] This astonishing true story would tell of alien contact and men in black, sowing the seeds of more recent science fiction, and the story of the Mothman itself has recently been made into a Hollywood movie. Back in the 1950s, however, before Keel met the Mothman, he met an old man in India who knew how to perform the rope trick.

In 1955, Keel travelled to India in search of adventure and magic and, at one point, a healer who lived on the outskirts of Secunderabad. Unable to find him, he walked to the top of a nearby hill, and there he apparently met an old man who called himself Vadaramakrishna. He 'went on to tell me several remarkable things', wrote Keel, but none more remarkable than the secret to the rope trick. Vadaramakrishna told Keel he had actually performed the trick in the olden days, and that its secret 'does not lie in the ground or in the rope, but in the air'. And the airy explanation that followed was described in full by Keel.

'The site of the performance was always in a valley between two hills or two rocky knolls,' he revealed, and an 'invisible wire was stretched from the summit of one hill, across the valley, to the summit of the other hill'. In those days, of course, wire had not been available to itinerant Indian performers, so they had constructed one from 'hairs woven together'. Alas, 'the hair ropes weren't completely invisible' so the trick 'was always performed at dusk'. When the rope was thrown in the air, a hook was secretly attached to the end, the hook in turn being at the end of a long thread which dangled over the horizontal support to 'a concealed spot where an assistant could pull it'. And pull it he did, causing the rope to rise upwards. A boy was then ordered to climb the rope, but '[h]e would act hesitant', as most people probably would if their only support was a thread dangling over a line made of hair. But 'the fakir would argue with him, even threaten him. Finally he would start to climb, hurtling back violent abuse', and when he got to the top, he would seem to vanish. 'There is a simple explanation,' Keel persisted, for '[t]orches or lanterns on the ground made the spectators night-blind when they looked up into the dark sky'.

So far, so good, but now the fakir 'would start up the swaying bouncing rope. When he reached the boy they would grapple and curse and seem to have a whale of a fight.' There they hung in the night sky, man and boy, supported by that increasingly taut line of human hair stretched between two hills, and having another argument. Perhaps it was about the additional weight, for 'the magician pulled from various sections of his clothing the parts of a freshly butchered animal (usually a large monkey)'. These were thrown to the ground 'while the boy screamed', and finally a 'head wrapped in a turban would strike the ground and bounce bloodily'. Under this additional misdirection, the boy climbed 'inside the baggy clothing of the magician, slipping his arms and legs into a special harness'. Back on the ground, of course, it was a relatively simple matter nonchalantly to replace the dismembered monkey with the boy, who reappeared in perfect health, wearing a convincing expression of relief on his face. This explanation, Keel remarked, was so simple that he would never have thought of it.

Many, on the other hand, would never have believed it, and might have wondered what to say to the old man they had met on the hill who had told them this implausible tale. But for Keel there was a different dilemma: 'Now that I had the

'**1** . . . the rope has been thrown into the air and invisibly hooked onto a wire . . . A hidden confederate hoists another, stabilising, wire over the main one.'

'**2** A small, lithe boy begins to climb the erect rope – and disappears.'

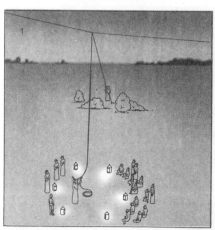

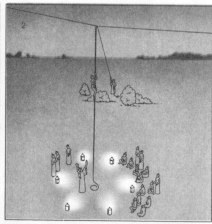

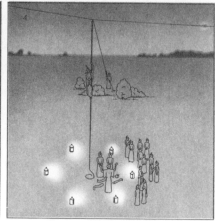

'**3** the fakir . . . climbs the rope himself, with a dagger. Then suddenly the horrified audience see the boy's limbs drop one by one to the ground.'

'**4** In fact, the "limbs" are those of a monkey – and the boy has also descended the rope with the fakir, strapped inside his robes. A few magic words and the boy is whole again.'

Keel's colourful explanation, though utterly impractical, continues to be presented to the public as the genuine secret of the rope trick.

basic secret of the trick in my hands,' he pondered, 'what to do with it? . . . I had to prove this *was* the secret.' And so he 'bought a long rope', and went in search of a suitable performing arena.

Eventually, he found a golf course with an old temple nearby, and 'rigged a network of black threads across the clearing in such a way that the rope would rise about fifty feet'. Ambitious as this was, he had no intention of performing the dismemberment part of the trick, much to the relief of the local monkey population. Indeed, though the rope would rise, 'no boy would climb it, but I thought it would make a convincing demonstration anyway'. With a boy assistant hidden in the old temple ready to 'operate the strings, an audience of [a]bout fifty reporters showed up . . . Then an incredible thing happened.' It began to rain, 'a high wind rose, and a monsoon cloudburst crashed around us'. Less confident about how weatherproof the true secret of the rope trick was, 'I tried to call the whole thing off. But the reporters were impatient.' This was a true dilemma, the 'threads were tangled in the bushes and . . . my assistant had fled . . . but I grimly went ahead . . . I managed to get the rope about four feet off the ground while everyone snickered. After my miserable efforts, the British correspondents threw me a contemptuous sneer and drove off.' Indian reviewers were more generous, however, and later reported only that 'Mr Keel's performance could not be called flawless', but he

THE ROPE TRICK
AT LAST.

Another theory involving the suffering of a monkey.

himself had to admit that '[i]f this fiasco had been enacted in New York, the papers there would have torn me to pieces'.[22]

Undaunted by his not quite flawless attempt to recreate the legendary feat, *sans* monkey, Keel continued on his Indian quest and met a native of Calcutta who knew something of Indian magic. He was known, in fact, as The World's Greatest Magician to anyone who read his publicity material – a title he humbly abbreviated to TWGM – and he told Keel that the 'rope trick is impossible'. According to Keel, when he told TWGM of the secret he had discovered, 'he only snickered'.[23] But after Keel left, TWGM stopped snickering and contacted the newspapers.

In 1960, TWGM announced to readers of *Modern Review*, a popular Indian periodical, that he had discovered the secret of the rope trick. He also wrote a paper for the Danish Society for Psychical Research, and published a book in English. In it, he boasted that he had 'made considerable researches to solve the mystery of the riddle of the "Indian rope trick". My findings have confirmed my belief that the rope trick is not a myth.' This apparent change of heart had been the result of studying, 'with a student's zeal and a magician's curiosity . . . the observations made by magicians of eminence and celebrity and the remarks and reports of men of rank and position all over the world'.[24] TWGM's solution, however, was almost identical to the one he had snickered at not so long ago, and which had already been published by Keel.[25] There were only minor differences in

TWGM's solution to the riddle. According to him, the thread of human hair was actually held at each end by an assistant standing on top of a nearby hill, and the performance was accompanied by the 'sound of weird Indian music', which contained a musical code that informed the assistants when to start pulling. Otherwise, it was the same bizarre method discovered in that serendipitous meeting at the top of a hill near Secunderabad. It worked, according to TWGM, because people back then were 'very much gullible'.[26]

But people were no longer gullible, and TWGM soon came under fire from his colleagues for publishing such an explanation. In a sea of accusations from fellow Indian magicians, TWGM was described as 'untruthful, baseless, and self-exalting', his method dismissed as 'fantastic and absurd', and the article condemned as 'an act of betrayal of our honoured past, an act of bamboozlement of our progressive present'. One magician complained that a Swede had been lured to India following TWGM's claim, and having 'come all the way from Sweden to see the rope trick, was greatly disappointed'. Such a false claim was therefore guilty of damaging India's 'aspiring development of tourism', and of 'injuring the reputation of India abroad'. In a booklet that claimed to have 'eliminated naked personal attacks', TWGM was called 'arrogant', and described as an 'emperor of publicity and not an emperor of magicians. His every step wades through a quagmire of self propaganda.'

In the absence of naked personal attacks, there was plenty of room for alternative theories, and these included both supernatural and natural explanations. One Indian magician who 'at the cost of my life, risked to travel the remotest parts of Kamrup in Assam . . . [and] crossed the Burmese border illegally . . . but in vain', concluded that 'the performer must possess that supernatural power by years of toilsome "sadhana"'. Others felt that nature might hold the key to the rising rope, and spoke of a special grass in the Terai regions of the Himalayas which stiffened when stretched, of a date palm in the Pakistan village of Faridpur that bowed in the sun but stood erect in the morning, and of a banyan tree by the ancient caves of Ellora whose roots became stiff at sunrise.[27]

And then, in the midst of the controversy, one man found it 'impossible to keep quiet', and finally provided 'the only sane solution'. He explained that the rope trick could be performed anywhere, anytime, 'miles from a tree or a house or a hill . . . in the morning, noon, or afternoon'. The conditions, in fact, were entirely irrelevant, providing one was aware of the secret mantra. There were naturally a couple of preparations, one of which was 'three weeks of preparatory penance. You can eat what you like, except fish, meat, and wife.' 'This is not a joke,' he assured readers, 'I am prepared to give the MANTRA to any honest magician who comes to me with evidence of his having completed the three weeks' penance. No fish, no meat, no wife. I am very sorry.'[28] Faced with such a sacrifice, and the obvious problem of providing the necessary evidence, people seem to have found the alternatives more attractive. Over the following years, the methods provided by Keel and TWGM have continued to be presented as genuine solutions, right up to the present day.[29] But at least one magician decided that if the rope trick could be performed without fish, meat or wife, it could be performed without monkey. According to him, '[t]he magician actually killed the boy. It's true. Cutting him to pieces was no act . . . the boy had a twin. For this reason, needing twins and having to kill one of them, the full trick was not performed very often.'[30] Not to mention the difficulty of rehearsing.

And these were 'normal' explanations, as opposed to paranormal ones. It is hardly surprising, therefore, that the latter emerged as well. There had, of course, always been the collective hypnosis theory. It had been the original theory in the *Chicago Tribune* story, had been proposed by various possessors of photographs which showed nothing happening, and might have been demonstrated in the Albert Hall if one were to take Dr Cannon seriously. The theory had continued to be touted in various forms, such as his lordship's mass hallucination theory induced by drugs, and despite the various scientific assurances that a crowd could not be hypnotised, there was the odd psychologist who persisted in the view that: 'fakirs mystify their onlookers by arousing, or inducing, in them a high degree of suggestibility and then causing them to hallucinate a boy climbing hand over hand up a rope and finally disappearing into the sky'.[31] The theory of collective hallucination, whether induced by drugs or a fakir, contradicted mainstream scientific thinking, so was, in that sense, paranormal, and further paranormal theories would emerge.

In the 1960s, both drugs and the paranormal played their part in maintaining the image of the mystic East, as the descendants of the earlier Western travellers continued to make the journey to India in search of what they felt was not available in the West. The Hippy Trail was, of course, quite different from the sailing routes of the East India Company, leading hundreds of thousands of Americans and Europeans down a road through Iran and Afghanistan which had not seen such business since before Moghul times. Like their predecessors, they went to purchase and consume locally grown products, and they went for spiritual reasons, but this time they sought neither profit nor converts. On the contrary, they had travelled east to experience and to learn. Much of that experience may have been in an altered state of consciousness – one pilgrim sat down with a sadhu, and took acid, at which point the sadhu 'then vanished, and turned into light. I became one with his breath, all form disappearing 'til I was in a pure state of *samadhi* [trance].'[32] Yet India, for these modern Western pilgrims, also seemed to fill a spiritual gap, and many sought a deeper alternative reality than hallucinogenics could provide. This demand was met by Indian gurus who offered their new flock a view of the universe that drew on ancient Indian philosophy, advised yogic meditation as an alternative form of inducing an altered state, and periodically performed miracles as demonstrations of the unreality of reality. The Beatles, most famously, came under the influence of Maharishi Mahesh Yogi, founder of the Transcendental Meditation movement, and practitioner of yogic flying. And for those who did not experience the India Trip, various aspects of Hinduism and Buddhism were exported to the West, and visitors returned home with tales of levitations and materialisations, all of them reinforcing the image of India as the home of spirituality, and of the wonder-working swami.

There was, as we know, nothing new about this, yet the most famous wonder of India remained a mystery, and the ongoing fascination with the notion that there were those in the East who possessed paranormal powers continued to provoke theories. Such a theory was put forward in the 1970s by Andrija Puharich, the biographer of Uri Geller, who believed that the Israeli's ability to bend cutlery was part of an extraterrestrial bid to help humankind.[33] He also believed that the rope trick was the result of mass hallucination induced via telepathy. His evidence for this was a report about an 'experiment' carried out by one Professor Pilcz, who claimed he had filmed a performance of the rope trick. In a long tradition of rope trick stories, the film showed no such performance, a fact confirmed by a colleague who saw the film, though as he had not seen the performance, his confirmation seems somewhat pointless. On the basis of third-hand knowledge, and an assurance about a film that showed nothing happening, Puharich concluded, 'we must assume that the hallucination was telepathically inspired'.[34] An equally plausible view was held by Ormond McGill, a magician with a keen interest in the mysticism of the East, who informed his readers that 'the magician creates and projects a concentrated thought form, which to the observers seems temporarily to exist as reality. Here, at last, is the real secret of the famous "East Indian Rope Trick".'[35]

The search for the secret has persisted up to the present day, and in the face of such challenges to the presently understood laws of nature, scientists have naturally continued to seek a scientific solution. Only a few years ago, New Scientist reported how two mathematicians had managed to perform 'the amazing Indian rope trick'.[36] What they had actually done was to vibrate the base of a vertical flexible wire at such a high frequency that it remained upright, an experiment that they were unable to replicate with a piece of rope. Physicists in Britain and the Netherlands have also managed to make a frog float in mid-air using giant magnetic fields. One of the researchers claimed that with a large enough magnet 'you could levitate a human', and he assured the public that the frog had not suffered any harm, but 'went back to its fellow frogs looking perfectly happy'. The team had also managed to levitate plants, grasshoppers and fish, though their subsequent condition was not reported.[37]

Such are the problems of trying to explain the inexplicable. It is not that explanations do not exist, it is rather that the ones that do are not entirely convincing. But the Indian rope trick is not unique in that respect, for it is only the most famous of the miraculous feats that have come to be associated with India, and explanations have been provided for all of them. Books on 'Hindu feats' became available throughout the twentieth century, explaining such classic Indian wonders as snake charming and 'the bed of nails', but also including a wide range of potentially dangerous demonstrations that were less obviously Indian. These were the books to read if you were interested in 'Driving a spike into your head', 'Eating a ball of fire', or the equally imaginatively entitled 'Car on head'. More delicate readers could relax at home with one of the more gentle 'feats of the yogi', such as 'hypnotizing a rabbit'. But anyone attempting the more adventurous pastimes would do well to read the instructions carefully. 'Chewing molten lead', for example, required a special compound that 'melts at approximately 160 degrees. If you wish a lower melting point, add to the above a small amount of quicksilver . . . When melted, this mixture may be poured on the tongue which, it goes without saying, must be moist with saliva.' And if the student was not convinced by that explanation, the following assurance of the author was given: 'Personally, I have never developed enough courage to try this, although several have told me it is OK.'[38]

One book entitled *Miraculous Hindu Feats* explained the secrets behind 'Branding oneself with a hot iron', 'Drinking acid' and 'Putting fingers in hot lead'. Anyone interested in performing this latter miracle was told in no uncertain terms:

> The hands must be devoid of *all* moisture. They *must* be perfectly dry. This can be done by 'washing' the hands with dry sand. Anything that will dry the hands will help, for the chief thing to remember and have is *dry hands*.[39]

But perhaps a second opinion might be sought before plunging one's hands into molten lead. 'The whole secret', another book assured its readers, 'lies in the fact the hands are washed before the performance . . . Do not dry the hands, but leave them still damp . . . The moisture prevents the hot metal from burning.'[40] Is it any wonder that the miracles of the East continue to be shrouded in a veil of mystery?

In the range of theories put forward to explain the Indian rope trick, there was, at least, something for everybody. One could choose between satanic agency or infanticide, between the views of a Jewish Nazi clairvoyant or those of an ambassador for psychic aliens, between chopping up a monkey or becoming a vegetarian celibate. One could seek out that mysterious smoke-producing substance, or one could use certain drugs of the East, which might not only provide the necessary smoke but might also help out with the other suggestions as well. They might not have been entirely convincing, but all of them contributed to the idea that the legend might have some sort of explanation. Yet none of them would have been suggested in the first place had it not been for the growing body of evidence that the trick had actually been performed. And looking beyond all the travellers' tales and hoaxes, there remained a substantial collection of individuals who claimed they really had seen a rope rise in India and a boy disappear at the top of it. But this remained inexplicable, unless performed on stage. So what did those witnesses really see?

The Real Indian Rope Trick

The Indian rope trick had come a long way, yet there seemed to be precious little reality to the world's most famous illusion. It had risen to fame following a newspaper story that the author had subsequently admitted was untrue, and had grown on the back of further hoax articles, fake photographs and the extravagant claims of publicity-conscious conjurors. India had been searched for the secret and large rewards had been offered, but despite the various efforts that had been made, the searches had been in vain and the rewards had remained unclaimed. A long history had been constructed that suggested the legend had been around for centuries, yet there was no evidence that the Indian rope trick of the twentieth century had been heard of until the end of the nineteenth. Occultists, scientists and eccentrics had joined the quest to provide a solution to the greatest mystery of the

Orient, and a wide range of implausible theories had been thought of, but none of them had been successfully demonstrated. The feeble attempts of Karachi and John Keel had shown only that, without the advantages of a stage, it was difficult to get a rope to rise more than a few feet. And yet the legend itself had continued to grow.

For when all the hoaxes and frauds and imaginative theories were placed aside, there remained a kernel of evidence upon which these various claims could feed, and which lent them an air of plausibility. For as the sceptics assured the public that the Indian rope trick did not exist, they were regularly interrupted by men and women who had claimed to have seen it with their own eyes. It was these eye-witnesses who brought a sense of reality to the legend. As in the case of Bigfoot and the Loch Ness Monster, it is ordinary people who bring a legend to life.

Not all of the witnesses were credible, of course. Even if one included the earlier stories that might have indirectly inspired Wilkie's story, they could hardly be taken as reliable evidence. Only a few could be regarded as eye-witness accounts, and scholars now doubt whether Ibn Battuta even visited China, while Emperor Jahangir's excessive drinking and smoking make his testimony somewhat dubious. But extraordinary accounts from centuries ago have rarely convinced a modern audience. What was different about the rope trick was that its witnesses included people who, as it was pointed out in 1934, 'may still be found alive in Britain to-day'.[1] These modern witnesses, seemingly untarnished by primitive superstition or the desire to dream up travellers' tales, appeared to be that much more credible to their contemporaries.

Naturally they could not all be trusted. Modern witnesses for the defence included the fictitious F. S. Ellmore, the wonderfully eccentric Dr Cannon, and the politically dubious Erik Jan Hanussen— all somewhat less than convincing. There were, on the other hand, more socially respectable individuals who had reportedly seen the rope trick. Earl Haig had supposedly seen it, according to the revelations of Sergeant Secrett, but not according to Lady Haig. And it was even claimed that HRH the Duke of Connaught watched a performance while 'sitting on his horse, and seemed highly interested'. But the Duke subsequently denied this, much to the delight of the arch-sceptic Elliot. 'I feel we are much indebted to His Royal Highness for graciously permitting this statement to be made,' Elliot humbly observed, before complaining on His behalf, '[i]t is little short of a scandal to bring members of the Royal family into the matter'.[2]

Given the dubious credentials of some of the witnesses, and such adamant denials among polite society, there was some doubt as to whether there were any reliable eye-witnesses at all. It was often said that 'none of us have met a person who actually saw it with his own eyes; the story never reaches us at first-hand, but always at second- or third-hand.'[3] Yet first-hand eye-witnesses did exist, as Elliot knew well, for he did his best to discredit them. Following the Committee meeting of 1934, an elderly lady wrote to him who was 'sorry to upset the views of the Occult Committee', but she had actually seen the rope trick performed, and 'at one of the displays I saw two monkeys chase each other up the rope'. In language he would not have used towards royalty, he sneered at this 'dear old lady . . . Can you beat that for a comic cut?' Meanwhile, another witness who had been billed in a newspaper as 'An Eye-Witness Who Could Not be Fooled' was dismissed by Elliot as someone who 'was taken in by a hoary old trick which every schoolboy conjurer knows how to do'.

But these individuals were not alone. In fact, from the heroic declaration of S. T. Burchett in 1904, to the publicity frenzy surrounding the Magic Circle challenge of 1934, there were at least forty first-hand eye-witnesses, including pillars of Anglo-Indian society such as Sir Ralph Sneyde Pearson. Sir Ralph had run the Imperial Forest Service, he had written such respected tomes as *A Further Note on the Antiseptic of Timber* and *Note on the Utilisation of Bamboo for Paper*, and he had been Lieutenant Governor of the North West Frontier Province. Lesser mortals had also reported seeing the rope trick and, as the sober *Chambers' Journal* pointed out, '[o]ne assumes that *all* the eye-witnesses of this Oriental illusion are neither liars nor victims of hallucinations'.[4] After all, S. T. Burchett had been described as 'absolutely honest' and others refused to be dismissed by the sceptics as the victims of hypnosis or hallucination. In the defiant words of one sergeant who had seen several years of service in the subcontinent, 'I saw it I tell you, I saw it!'

Even the sceptics had to conclude that the witnesses had seen something. John Nevil Maskelyne had felt that '[s]o many stories have been told about this trick that I felt sure there must be some foundation for them', though he had suggested a trick method which had failed to convince even fellow sceptics.[5] Elliot, on the other hand, admitted that '[t]here is probably some starting point for each of these stories . . . [but t]he rest is to be attributed to an overactive imagination combined with a defective memory, a poor power of observation and a desire for the limelight'.[6] But if they had not seen the rope trick, what had they seen? For whatever it was they had witnessed was the basis for their testimony, and it was their testimony that kept the legend alive, that made it real. In a sense, whatever they had seen was the *real* Indian rope trick. And perhaps that could be found, not by searching in India, but by looking more closely at the source of the legend's reality: eye-witness testimony itself. Somewhere in that mass of memories, the spectacle they had really seen might yet be revealed.

There was, for example, a witness who signed himself 'Percy M'. According to Percy, a boy 'began climbing up [a twine] till he vanished from sight when the twine came hurtling down and settled on the ground. The man . . . with a sword approached a coffin-shaped basket which had its lid down. He jabbed the sword into the basket at different places, then lifted the lid and stepped back, when the boy . . . jumped out of the basket.'[7] Percy reported this in 1934, but he claimed he had seen it in 1884. Fifty years on, it is reasonable to suppose he might have got some of his details mixed up, and the last part he described sounds for all the world like the end of the basket trick. It so happens that Percy was not alone, for several other witnesses described a boy disappearing at the top of a rope, then reappearing inside a basket after it had been stabbed at with a sword. So it seems rather likely these witnesses combined elements of the basket trick with their memory of the rope trick, creating a more impressive illusion overall. This, of course, does not tell us about the first part of the account, but then not all of the witnesses waited fifty years to tell their tale.

It was a mere seventeen years after the event when a certain Mr Curtis reported seeing the rope trick, and his version was less elaborate than that of Percy. According to Curtis, '[t]he boy climbed up the rope and disappeared. It seemed quite five minutes before he reappeared at the top of the rope.'[8] Relatively simple stuff, perhaps, yet still a feat that conjurors were unable to reproduce without a stage. But then seventeen years remain a considerable time, and most of us would trust more recent memories. Take, for example, Mr Hedges who reported in 1921 that he had seen the trick during the Great War, and who claimed only that '[t]he boy climbed the rope and came down'. His four-year-old memory of the trick led him to conclude that 'the performance as I saw it was not as elaborate as those which I believe take place'.[9]

This, it turns out, was a general pattern throughout the eye-witness accounts. The longer the period between when the trick had been seen and when it had been reported, the more impressive the account of it. A few years ago, a clever psychologist called Dr Wiseman, along with an equally wise and manly (but humble) colleague, analysed all the accounts containing the necessary details. The correlation between the delay in reporting the trick and the impressiveness of the account is so strong that the odds of the two *not* being linked are about one in two thousand.[10] If, as the evidence suggests, the witnesses were exaggerating over time, then what was it that they had seen? For that we must look to the eye-witness account that appeared soonest after the event. This account was only two years old, and the witness himself later admitted that he had exaggerated. Better still, he had actually taken a photograph of the performance. If the exaggeration theory is correct, then this is a photograph of what the witnesses really saw – the real Indian rope trick. The name of the witness who took the photograph was Lieutenant Holmes, and his photograph was the one that had appeared in 1919, a photograph of a boy balancing on his stomach on top of a pole.

The pole-balancing feat was a traditional juggling feat in India, as in other parts of the East, and we know it was performed alongside the basket trick. In the 1860s, one of Charles Dickens's journals reported a performance of an Indian juggler: 'holding a staff in his waistband and letting a brother juggler swarm up it and lay himself all abroad on the top . . . the body balanced only on one part of the stomach – after these and other kindred displays he comes to the finale of all: the girl and the basket'.[11] When William H. Seward, former US Secretary of State, had visited India in the 1870s, he had remembered seeing 'a man climb up a pole sixty feet high, standing in open air, and when he reached the top he disappeared'. And in 1889, the *Times of India* reported an eye-witness account of a performance of Indian juggling in Bengal. 'A boy was called, who held upright a long bamboo, up which the man climbed to the top, whereupon we lost sight of him . . . Then there fell on the ground before us the different members of a human body, all bloody.' This was also reported in the British press, yet nobody mentioned the Indian rope trick at the time because, in 1889, the legend had not yet entered the popular imagination. A few years later, however, it was possible to confuse a visual memory of a boy climbing a pole with a well-known story about a boy climbing a rigid rope. When an early twentieth-century witness, several years after he had seen the event, recalled, 'I saw it stand up straight; a small boy climbed up to the top, balanced

Indian jugglers performing without the aid of a rope. Compare this with the Holmes photograph on page 104.

on his stomach and disappeared', he was speaking of the Indian rope trick.[12]

And so, in retrospect, it seems that what Lieutenant Holmes photographed was the real Indian rope trick after all. It is just that the legendary rope trick did not employ a rope. The legend itself rose to fame following a hoax and was perpetuated by witnesses who saw a trick but no rope. The rope they did not see did not rise, and the boy they did see did not vanish. Such are the humble foundations on which legends can be built. And though this was a legend about the East, it was one that was fabricated in the West. It might be said of stories of the rope trick 'that the Oriental imagination is busily at work here', but that was only a reflection of Western notions of India as the home of a credulous people.[13] The legend of the rope trick was born in the West, and was fed not by the Oriental imagination, but by how the West imagined the Orient. In a modern West that had dis-enchanted itself in the name of science and progress, a magical East was required to satisfy the deeper human need for wonder. The West needed the Indian rope trick, and perhaps it still does. After all, the image of the mystic East is still with us, and as long as the human imagination is capable of transforming the mundane into something more wonderful, the world will continue to be enchanted, and legends will never die.

The suspense of disbelief: Alfred Hitchcock fears that this is the end of the rope trick.

EPILOGUE: THE LEGEND CONTINUES . . .

(Udupi, Karnataka, India, 1997)

It was a private bus, and seemed to be in competition not only with other buses on the route, but with every animate object in its path. To the left of our fearless driver was a figure of Ganesh, the elephant-headed god of many things, including travel. The figure was surrounded by flashing lights that suggested an air of divine panic, giving the impression that even he could not help at this speed. There was little time to observe small-town India as it flew by, and precious little space to permit a view. Bus stops were treated with pit-stop efficiency, and the Bollywood music that thundered through the loudspeakers reinforced the sense of urgency. We nevertheless arrived late, and nobody seemed either concerned or surprised.

I was in Udupi, home of the Sri Ananthasana temple, birthplace of the *masala dosa*, and the venue for the largest magic convention in India. The temple is associated with several miracles, including a reported feeding of the multitude, and the convention began promptly with six hundred delegates filing into the dining hall to be fed with vegetarian thalis served on banana leaves. For the first few minutes I was watched intently by Indian magicians curious whether a European sleight-of-hand expert, as they supposed me to be, was capable of eating with his fingers. By the end of the first day I had been given twenty-seven business cards, and had apologised nineteen times for bringing only eight of my own. By way of apology, I had agreed to be photographed with every magician who asked, autographed every programme I was handed, and never looked surprised when each of these eager fans had subsequently asked my name.

A magic convention is a bizarre event in any country, and this was to be no exception. There were the magic dealers, who make their living from selling tricks to magicians. Ideally, since many magicians are lazy, such tricks require no practice, relying instead on a gimmick, a secret device that makes the trick work, and of which the audience is completely unaware. In practice, however, such tricks are not very impressive and are rarely performed, which is why many magicians' drawers are full of strange-looking devices of which, since they have never been used, the audience is completely unaware. The Indian magic dealers resembled those in Blackpool or Las Vegas: more skilful and experienced than most of their customers, thus capable of making a simple trick look more impressive than it will later, when the customer practises once in front of the mirror, then promptly consigns it to the drawer of mystery. One man insisted on demonstrating a plastic box that could make a coin disappear, another directed me towards a large wooden rabbit that was available at a very reasonable price because one of its ears was damaged. Cigarette manipulation, no longer fashionable in the United States, was on display in one corner, as a Gold Flake vanished and reappeared in ways a Marlboro once enjoyed. There were boxes painted with rabbits emerging from top hats, waistcoats embroidered with images of playing cards and magic wands, artificial flowers that compress small enough to be concealed within a suspicious-looking tube, and more silk handkerchiefs than I had ever seen before. Over the following days, isolated from the real world, I lost count of how many silk handkerchiefs were produced from thin air or thick boxes, of how many bunches of plastic flowers appeared from suspicious-looking tubes, though I managed to count nineteen doves and thirty-six umbrellas.

This degree of repetition is one reason why few people, other than magicians, attend full-length magic shows, and is by no means peculiar to India. Stage magicians all over the world endlessly produce and vanish playing cards, silk handkerchiefs, candles and doves, and few fully appreciate the law of diminishing marginal returns. How many handkerchiefs must a man make appear before they call him a magician? The answer, my friends, is one, but the average is over a dozen, and their colours invariably match those of the national flag, into which they transform at the end of the routine. But Indian magic was not always like this. For centuries, visitors to India reported the most extraordinary feats of levitation, snake charming, burial and resurrection. Indian jugglers gained a reputation for being the greatest magicians on earth. In the last century, as Westernised stage magic became more common in India, the traditional itinerant jugglers declined. But in Udupi, they were there, and an excited audience of thirty thousand gathered in the midday heat to watch them.

The audience had arrived by diverse modes of transport. They had caught a local bus from town, walked many miles from surrounding villages, travelled from the north in air-conditioned and non-a/c coaches, and flown from Europe and America. Now they stood as equals in the midday heat, trying to decide which wonder to watch, but the choice was not always theirs. As a performance of the basket trick began, several hundred spectators around me moved closer, trying to decide my destination for me – but I had not come to India for the basket trick. When I emerged from that crowd, another large group was heading to the left to watch the levitation of a small boy, and it took several minutes to resist their enthusiasm. Directly ahead was the patch of ground beneath which a man was about to be buried alive, and this time it was impossible to argue with the masses. On the way, we passed two men waiting to demonstrate hook-swinging. Four large hooks already pierced each back, and one each calf, but they were not to be suspended from the poles until after the resurrection, and they passed the time in no apparent discomfort, calmly reading the newspaper.

There was no obvious way of getting near to the burial site, the mob was so eager and closely knit, and by the time I had found a viewpoint on top of a nearby ambulance, the man was already underground. For half an hour or so, we watched the ground, and those who could not see waited anyway. Meanwhile, the arena looked remarkably similar to several patches of ground nearby that nobody took any interest in, and those of us who had not actually seen the man being buried began to wonder whether we were victims of a hoax. Yet the competition for a view was so fierce that nobody dared leave. So we stood, watching nothing happen, while countless others struggled to get a better view. When it became clear that the man was about to resurface, the crowd became frantic. Those of us who had suspected a hoax grew less cynical, but were particularly keen to see the man emerge from the ground we had been watching for so long. Those who had arrived in time to see him being buried felt their punctuality entitled them to see the finale, while the growing numbers who had not yet seen the ground began to realise this might be their last chance. The circle of spectators around the patch of ground began to close in, despite the entreaties of the assistants and the threats of the police. For several minutes it seemed as if the man would emerge from his grave only to be buried alive in a stampede of curiosity. It was the cheers of those who made it to the front that informed the majority that our hero was safe, though most of us never saw him. Nevertheless, we would boast later of how we had witnessed a miracle.

Above the heads of another crowd, two horizontal poles rotated slowly. Below the poles hung two horizontal men facing the ground, the skin on their backs and calves tested by gravity. Below them, their newspapers lay on the ground, and it seemed as if they were still reading them as they passed above with each new revolution. A few hundred yards away, an eighty-year-old Gujarati slowly allowed a scorpion to emerge from his mouth. Then a snake. This circle of spectators were less keen to close in, though when he transformed a brick into two huge cobras, it was several seconds before they dispersed, the paralysis of wonder delaying the repulsion of fear. And yet I had not come to Udupi for any of this.

We gathered on the beach near Udupi for a performance of the rope trick, wondering what we were about to see. Among the vast audience were the hook-swingers, but they were no longer reading. To the left was a man I did not recognise, his clothes still covered in earth. To the right, a certain octogenarian Gujarati was being allowed a surprising amount of space. Centre-stage was Ishamuddin, a Delhi street magician, addressed the enormous crowd in Hindi, though most would have spoken Kannada and some English. It was nevertheless clear to all that there was no stage, nothing overhead, and the performance area was almost completely surrounded. The rope was about twenty feet long, and was placed inside a basket. Ishamuddin began to play a pipe and, in a rough simulation of snake charming that has often been associated with the rope trick, one end of the rope emerged at the top of the basket. Slowly it rose to a height of five feet. A moment later, it began to descend.

The crowd seemed genuinely astonished (that they had travelled so far to see this), and a moment of uncertainty followed in which thousands of people from several countries considered how best to deal with the situation. The locals reassured themselves that they had wasted only a few hours, and could look down on those who had travelled many miles from surrounding rural areas. The latter, in turn, could find solace in the frustration of those who had travelled all the way from the north. And there were, of course, the foreigners to make everyone else feel a little better. But the embarrassed looks we exchanged were soon interrupted by the sound of Ishamuddin's pipe, which began to play again, and which enticed the rope upwards once more. It rose to five feet, then to ten, and finally to almost twenty. There, against the setting sun, it was an impressive sight – and then the boy walked forward. Some words were exchanged between the two performers, though few of us understood, and Ishamuddin pointed upwards. The boy took hold of the rope with both hands, and slowly he began to climb, higher and higher . . .

(Kovalam beach, South India, later)

The anticipation in Paradise is becoming unbearable. In an hour, they will arrive, and those whose role it is to serve them are waiting. It has been months since the last season, the monsoon has been and gone, and the sun that draws them here is waiting too. For the moment, it is not at all clear how many there will be, but that has not prevented the rumours. Some of those who wait have heard that the planes will be empty, that this will be a bad season, and that all these months of waiting will have been in vain. Others have heard quite the opposite, that many hundreds are due to arrive on the first plane, which seats only 268 passengers. In an hour, they will discover that they have been too pessimistic, or too optimistic, and that there will be 268 of them, as there were last year. The new arrivals will be driven from the airport by luxury coach, and guided to one of a handful of chosen hotels on the beach. Their luggage will be more than ample for a long stay, though their stay will not be long. These enormous suitcases will be carried on the heads of porters, who will negotiate the narrow steep path from the road to the hotel with intense focus and surprising grace. Two weeks later, they will be carried back up the hill, most of their contents having remained there throughout the fortnight, entirely unnecessary but packed just in case. The headloaders who have to carry this unnecessary weight do not know how unnecessary it is, but are glad of the available work. In that sense, the cautious packing of Europeans is not without a purpose.

Meanwhile, the beach-workers are ready for them. The lunghi men, the fruit women, and the cigarette boys are poised. When the first dazed tourists decide to bravely explore the beach, they will be confronted with a mild stampede of overpriced cheap goods: lunghis of the cheapest dyed cotton; foreign cigarettes that have been dumped on Asia because they are not mild enough to be sold in the West; beach mats that are tough enough to scratch the skin but cannot last a week. These will be foisted on unsuspecting first arrivals, still jet-lagged, not yet used to the currency, virgins in the market. There is a rumour here that a boy once sold a beach mat to a tourist for one thousand rupees on the first day, though nobody remembers his name. One such sale a day during the season would make a man unspeakably rich, but one a week would be a comfortable living for the rest of the year. Every new arrival represents that possibility, a source of unimaginable wealth in search of a beach mat. It is rumoured that it costs millions of rupees to fly here so that one can sit on this beach, so a thousand rupees for the mat that one sits on does not seem so implausible. But they are reasonable

men, and will offer a good price, a special price for you
because you are from England, or Germany, or Switzerland,
and will accept five hundred, or four hundred, or – last
price – three hundred. OK, two hundred, but now they have
made a loss, one hundred and fifty not possible, but only
because you are a friend. It is a good mat, it will last many
years, and if you need another one next week, you will get a
special price. What about a lunghi, cigarettes, grass, good
grass, a coconut? The next day, the unsuspecting tourist will
realise how much she paid for the beach mat, will think of the
price both times she sits on it and scratches her skin, then she
will sit on her towel and wonder why she wanted a beach mat.
For the next two weeks, she will be offered many beach mats
but she will not be caught again. The beach mat boy will have
one hundred and fifty rupees to feed his family for a day or
two, and the next day will be out again in search of a living
from now beach-wise tourists who will refuse to pay more
than ten rupees for anything, feeling it is they who are the
victims here.

In the evenings the victims will parade past the long line of
restaurants on the beach, proudly strolling behind their
enormous bellies in beachwear that can barely keep up. They
will exercise enormous discretion in their choice of
restaurant, the only exercise they engage in these days, for this
is the main event of the evening. This is also the case for those
who wait for them, who greet every belly as a close friend,

displaying the fresh fish that might fill them and hurling polite entreaties in broken English towards those who follow behind. No tourist can pass without running this gauntlet of eager restaurant workers pleading in every manner possible to come inside, stretching their vocabulary to its limit. Like the fishermen who supply them, these waiters wait for the next catch, hoping to reel in a large one with a strong line.

Once inside, there will be the ritual of choosing a table, a process, it is rumoured, that once lasted several days, though nobody can remember exactly when or where that was. Once seated, some of the newcomers will haggle over the prices on the menu until they learn it does not work like that. As they await their chosen feast, they will be offered all manner of unwanted wares by those who pass by with small bellies. Cheap and rough cigarettes will be pushed towards people who look like potential customers because they have just begun their box of duty-frees. Women will approach customers eating fruit salad to see if they would like a pineapple. Sunglasses will be shown to people who obviously like sunglasses because they are wearing them in the evening, an indication that these are being worn to be looked at rather than looked through, and that those who model them are not interested in cheap imitations. One man walks endlessly back and forward asking tourists if they would like their sandals cleaned, but as he speaks no English, nobody is sure what they are declining. Another man holds aloft a large wooden elephant, wearing a smile of unwarranted optimism, since nobody is interested in a large wooden elephant.

After sunset, it is quieter, and the well-fed look out to the barely visible sea, wondering why they are still not happy. It is a mixed bunch. Elderly European women trying to look discreet with the young Indian boys they accompany, but with whom they have nothing to talk about. Middle-aged European men with Indian boys, less self-conscious because they are less obvious, though only just. There are more conventional couples, of course, young, in love and falling out, old, still in love and long fallen out, here to share new experiences with each other or to experience new distractions from each other. Families, the father pretending he knows how it works over here, the mother outwardly smiling because she knows she does not, inwardly smiling because she knows he does not, children not smiling at all. Groups that seem hard to categorise because they are odd in number, uneven in gender balance, of disparate ages, except for one group who smile continually but never laugh – Christian volunteers are to be found everywhere. Then a beach puppy appears, and the waiter starts to play with it, rolling about on the floor in full knowledge that everyone is looking. And everyone smiles, even the children, but not for as long as the Christians.

And there are others too, solitary but not alone, trying to look content without smiling, even at the cute puppy. They are travellers, not tourists, and some of them have been travelling for a long time. They have been to many places and seen many things, but they have learned not to smile. They have seen it all before, and if they have not, they have seen something similar elsewhere, most probably somewhere you have not been to. Smiling is for tourists, not travellers, who are in the difficult business of travelling without having fun. Their task is to stay in the cheapest hotels, eat at the cheapest cafés, travel on the cheapest ticket. Their mission is to do as many places as possible, and do them cheaper than their fellow travellers. They did Rajasthan for a month, did the holy lake, did the camel trekking, they did all the stuff in the book, but they went off the beaten track to do some places they knew others would not do, and for all the stuff they did, they did not smile. They did, of course, smoke a lot of grass, the grass is good here, but not as good as some other place you have not been to, and much cheaper than here. But then this place is really touristy. And there follows a well-trodden list of remarks about tourists, not travellers, many of them true, none of them fair. Because what the travellers, not tourists, fail to see, despite all the places they have done, is that they are tourists too, only cheaper. Not poorer, but cheaper, as they haggle over five rupees with hawkers on the beach, explaining to people who make their living from selling coconuts that they are travellers, not tourists, and do not have any money. They have travelled half way around the world in search of bargains from the poor. Privileged children of middle-class families, conforming to the safest of rebellions, dressing down, washing infrequently, in search of a sense of poverty. They are not here on holiday, they are here for a year out, to see what things are like on the other side, to empathise with the poor, but not to tip them. But the poor do not empathise back, they see only tourists, tourists who do not tip. They wonder why they dress so badly, why they pretend to be short of money, why they do not smile when they are on holiday.

Then there is the walking man. He has been here for many years, and he has spent much of that time walking without going very far. Adorned in a pair of swimming trunks so small that they do not deserve the plural, and in which he never swims, his skin is dark and wrinkled, his hair long and bleached. He carries a pouch of tobacco in one hand, a packet of skins in the other, there being insufficient material for pockets, as he walks back and forward along the beach for hours on end, stopping occasionally to skin up and examine the sea, without going too close. Perhaps a philosopher, indifferent to academic status, searching for *satori* in postcard paradise. Never speaking, only looking, eyes calm, body relaxed, armed with all the enigma that calm and silence provide. All this enigma is lost one day, when he is heard to remark, in a Welsh accent, that the brunette ahead has a nice pair of tits. And with these magic words, the philosopher has vanished, to be replaced by a letch, the sudden transformation of one human being into another.

It is, of course, that much easier for the letch than the philosopher to find what he seeks. Many have come to Paradise looking for happiness, but only the shallow will be truly successful. Those who seek the conventional ingredients of weather, scenery, food and cold beer are not disappointed, and dutifully inform those back home of their success, now via email rather than a postcard. But those who seek something deeper will have to work harder and for less reward. India, of course, is a spiritual place, and many have come on spiritual quests, to find themselves, to meditate, to temporarily reject the material West between lying on the beach in the afternoon and watching a video in the evening. This demand for Eastern spirituality is only the most recent form of Orientalism, and is met by swamis, ashrams and early evening yoga classes. Ayurvedic treatments promise cures for arthritis, obesity and migraine to the stiff, fat and celibate, while the healthy-bodied seek inner peace. Solutions to every conceivable problem are sought, but the answers are found to be ambiguous. One young woman says that she is not sure why she came here, she had somehow been drawn to India, but now she was here, she understood, though she could not explain it in words. I asked her what she was talking about, but she genuinely did not know. She began three different sentences, finished none of them, shrugged her shoulders, faintly smiled, looked somewhere in the distance, then announced with all the profundity she could muster that we in the West were obsessed with having to explain things, something she found unnecessary as well as difficult. And I supposed I could explain why I had come to India, what I was looking for, when I would find it? I told her I had come for a miracle, that was what I was looking for, and as for when I would find it, it was only a matter of time. Then I left, thinking it was her who was weird.

I woke up slightly dazed, looked out of the window and saw what seemed like a long pole. It had climbed slowly upwards already, and now it was no longer possible to see precisely where it ended. Then a man climbed up to the top and, after a while, I could not see him. There were some strange noises, then something fell abruptly to the ground. As it fell, I could not help thinking it looked like a man's head. Several more objects fell to the ground, and I got up, dressed quickly, and went out to investigate. By the time I had got there, the man was standing before me, in perfect health.

To be awoken by the sound of falling coconuts is not so pleasant an experience as the phrase suggests. In any case, these had not so much fallen as been pushed. The coconut man had called. Every two or three months, the kymani, or climbing man, pays a visit to those fortunate enough to have a palm tree in their garden, and Lucky Villa, where I was staying, had two.[1] For 15 rupees, the kymani climbs a tree and cuts down the ripe coconuts. Last year, the brother of this man fell from a tree and was killed. This year he had to climb both trees in the garden. Sooraj, the house owner, did not pay him 30 rupees, but seven coconuts, five rupees per nut, plus a tip, because Sooraj is not a traveller. As another coconut fell from the second tree, hitting the ground like a meteor, Sooraj informed me that a coconut never lands on a man. One of those statements designed to put you at ease but, since the thought had never occurred to you, it only reminds you what a dangerous world you are living in. The kymani descended the tree, showed me a coconut, and said 'coconut'. Unsure why he was telling me this, but confronted by a man holding a large knife who severs nuts for a living, I nodded. I have never particularly liked coconut milk, but I kept drinking, nodding and saying 'mmm' till he had gone, at which point I could relax for two or three months. After a cup of coffee, primarily to get the taste out of my mouth, I went to see a swami.

It was a thirty-minute drive, I was told, which meant I had at least an hour to sit back and enjoy the continuous stream of oncoming traffic, and to suspect things were going a little too smoothly. It was Sabu, the taxi driver, who had told me about the swami. He had learned that I was here in search of an extraordinary feat, and thought the swami might be able to help. There had been no suggestion that the swami could perform the rope trick — on the contrary, he specialised in materialisations — but this was nevertheless a rare opportunity to witness a genuine Indian swami miracle. In any case, I had time, I needed time. As we swerved our way through the seemingly random traffic-pedestrian relationship of Thiruvananthapuram city centre, I thought about what I had seen in Udupi. The memory remained fairly fresh, of the rope rising almost twenty feet, of the boy slowly climbing up the rope in front of a setting sun. And then, of course, my thoughts were interrupted by Sabu, who announced we had arrived.

A disciple assured me that the swami had performed many miracles, and would be happy to perform one for me, but not at the moment. He was in a meeting, and would not be available for some time. Tomorrow would be fine. Meanwhile, here was some reading matter. The swami was, I read, the embodiment of love and mercy, and the head of a charitable trust. It was, in fact, two days later that I finally met the swami, and I still had the taste of coconut milk in my mouth. He assured me that there was nothing miraculous about miracles, and that anyone could perform them. The materialisation of an object was not the production of something from nothing, merely the transformation of matter, like water into ice, like the birth of a child. Of course, he could demonstrate this, but it was not important. In any case, he had a meeting to go to. Meanwhile, here was a banana and a piece of confectionery. These were not materialised, but openly removed from a box containing bananas and confectionery, and were presented with a nonchalance that suggested they were a standard souvenir. I was, however, welcome to come to the meeting and, in the hope he might perform a miracle, I accepted.

The meeting, not being in English, was a complete mystery. The swami sat cross-legged on a stool, dressed in violet silk, looking very much like the embodiment of love and mercy. His beard was long, but not as long as his smile, which had begun when I had entered the room and was now into its tenth minute. It was not the smile of a born-again Christian, less smug, more content, and he looked more relaxed than anyone I had ever seen. His hands were immaculately clean, his nails manicured, and his gestures gentle. His hair seemed surreally perfect, and I wondered whether he trimmed his eyebrows. To the right, a ten-foot cardboard cut-out of the swami was resting against the wall, surrounded in fairy lights which were thankfully, for the moment, switched off. Leaning there against the wall, it seemed more relaxed than the swami, until he began to chant, when a whole new level of calmness came over him. Like an infectious yawn, it began to have an effect, and I felt myself sink slightly into the chair, but was abruptly awoken when the dozen or so disciples in the room, whom I had completely forgotten about, began to chant back. This, I decided, was the moment that a miracle might happen, and as the others relaxed, I sat up and studied those immaculate hands for any sign of palming. They were empty. Watching with an intensity that seemed entirely inappropriate to the company, I waited for the moment he would drop his hand out of sight to obtain the object for materialisation. Then the chanting stopped, and there appeared to be a question-and-answer session. Somewhat disappointed, I sighed a little too heavily, drawing the attention of a nearby disciple, who seemed to be glad I was finally relaxing. Or perhaps he could see that, in all the excitement, my banana had become slightly out of shape, and my piece of confectionery was staining my white trousers. Either way, it seemed an appropriate time to leave.

As I left, another disciple seemed surprised that I no longer wanted to meet the swami, until I explained that I had a meeting. In an attempt to be polite, I told her I might come back later, at which point she suggested midday, and before I had got to the door, she had extracted a promise. Partly out of guilt, partly optimism, I was back there at noon sharp. The swami was, of course, at a meeting, and I was, of course, welcome to attend. An hour later, I was genuinely bored and a little annoyed, having been kept waiting for that time by a meeting that rarely spoke, and then in a language I could not understand. The smiles now seemed bland and weak, and the cardboard cut-out leaning against the wall with its dormant fairy lights now looked ridiculous. As I walked out of the building, the embodiment of impatience and resentment, I began to look forward to lunch. Five minutes later, our car left, and a minute after that, it stopped. Three disciples were now waving frantically at Sabu who, for a moment, seemed to suspect I had stolen something. It appeared that the swami's meeting had finally ended, and he was waiting for me. I told Sabu I would be back in ten minutes.

Ten minutes later, I was back in the car, holding another banana and piece of confectionery in my right hand, and a polished stone in my left. The latter had materialised, or rather it had been transformed from surrounding matter, before my eyes. He had been in his room, sitting cross-legged and wearing the same smile as before, or at least one that was very similar. He had explained again that miracles were unimportant, and that there was nothing miraculous about them. His empty right hand had dropped behind his right knee, and emerged a moment later in a fist, though such details are, like the miracle itself, unimportant. He had raised his fist in the air, then opened it dramatically to reveal a polished stone. I had looked the embodiment of love and mercy directly in the eyes, and asked him where it had come from, and he had repeated that it was no more than the transformation of matter, like water into ice, like the birth of a child. He had repeated that there was nothing miraculous about it, and I had believed him.

On the way back, it was necessary to visit a travel agent, not necessarily a Christian travel agent, but that is what the sign said. On the desk was an old newspaper cutting proudly displayed in a picture frame. The headline read, 'Face of Jesus Photographed over Somalia'. Beneath the headline was a black and white picture of a cloudy sky over Somalia, over which the image of a man, possibly Robert Powell, had been unconvincingly imposed. A US marine, who had supposedly witnessed this surreal cloud arrangement, was quoted as saying, 'I'm not the most religious guy in the world, but I recognise Jesus Christ when I see him.'[2] The Christian travel agent assured me that, if you believed in God, anything was possible, but getting a reservation at this short notice was out of the question.

That night, the endless optimism of the remote control scanned the bottomless pit of cable television for anything of value. But, like the hawkers on the beach, quantity was all that was available, which no doubt explains why many others stop for a while at the miracle channel. There, a succession of middle-aged American men deliver a long line of polished pitches wearing a series of conspicuous hairpieces. They heal the sick and promise material wealth to subscribers, but never explain why a miracle-worker needs a wig. The following day, the newspaper reported that a Godman in Rajasthan had confessed to 'murder and sexual escapades'. Believers were reportedly shocked to hear that a follower of the seventy-year-old Godman had threatened to expose his sexual exploits with over a hundred followers. While many men of that age might be glad of such publicity, the Godman, who was not the embodiment of love and mercy, had 'wielded a hatchet and sliced her head'. Meanwhile, in the territory that borders to the north, a police sub-inspector had been 'attacked with swords and sticks and his injuries are grievous'.[3] And here, in Paradise, there was an ongoing controversy over compensation for a boy who was allegedly tortured by the police. In the midst of such realities, no wonder legends survive.

A legend is very much like an illusion, more interesting and invariably more attractive than reality. It represents what might be rather than what is, and demands only the suspension of disbelief. Like an illusion, it is less an alternative to reality than a short break from it, a two-week holiday in Paradise after several hard months in the real world. We have always needed legends, and they have always provided that escape route: cords have always risen into the air, providing access to the heavens; the dead have always been resurrected, symbolising the survival of the human spirit. That is why the legend of the Indian rope trick, like the trick itself, has risen to great heights, and why, when it has been apparently killed off, it has been restored to life. The rise of the Indian rope trick is a victory of imagination over reality. Like a brochure advertising holidays in Paradise, it is not supposed to be taken literally. Yet it shows, like the memory of the holiday itself, that a mundane experience can be transformed over time into something more wonderful.

Meanwhile, in Paradise, it is quiet again. Those who have come are sleeping, and those who serve them are dreaming of what they will sell them tomorrow. The beach is empty now, so unlike the beach near Udupi, where a rope rose into the air, and where a boy climbed up the rope. The darkness facilitates the imagination, and makes room for the memory. I can hear the sound of Ishamuddin's pipe playing again, and see the rope being enticed upwards once more. It rises to five feet, then to ten, and finally to almost twenty. There against the setting sun, it is an impressive sight, and then the boy walks forward. Some words are exchanged between the two performers, though few of us understand, and Ishamuddin points upwards. The boy takes hold of the rope with both hands, and slowly he begins to climb, higher and higher . . . and when he reaches the top, the boy disappears.

NOTES

Welcome to the Notes. Most readers will not bother to look at these, which makes me wonder whether it is worth bothering with them in the first place. And then you come along, and make it all worthwhile. Thanks. Just by reading this, you are placing yourself among the top 10 per cent of readers – doesn't that make you feel good? Anyway, let us move on to the reference for the first quotation.

Chapter 1

1 Col. Henry Yule, *The Book of Ser Marco Polo* (London, 1873), vol. 1, p. 292. Many have since claimed that Marco Polo reported seeing the rope trick, despite there being no evidence for the claim. According to the *Occult Review* back in 1905, 'Marco Polo was profoundly impressed with it' (p. 292); Will Blyth wrote that it had been 'described by Marco Polo' (*Magic Circular*, 15, 1921, p. 129), and the error has continued right up to the present year (John Booth, *Extending Magic beyond Credibility* (Tahoma, 2001), p. 211). These mistakes probably followed, directly or indirectly, from a misreading of Yule's book, which contains notes (written by Yule, not Marco Polo) that describe stories related to the rope trick legend. These stories are discussed in chapter 8 of this book. Meanwhile, it is worth pointing out that this is precisely the sort

of sloppy history that has plagued the legend of the Indian rope trick. If only people were more like you, and read notes properly, the world would be a better place.

2 Rev. Samuel Lee, *The Travels of Ibn Batuta; translated from the abridged manuscript copies, preserved in the public library of Cambridge* (London, 1984), p. 162. This was first published in 1829. This might be a good time to point out that these notes may sometimes cover more than one extract or point. In this case, a few extracts are being used, and the note indicator appears after the last of these. This is simply to avoid repeating the same reference each time, or cluttering the main text with endless note indicators. If a quotation does not have an indicator at the end, just follow the text until you get to the next note, and you should find the reference there. It might also be worth adding that notes can be used to provide additional information that is not felt crucial to the main narrative. Which, I suppose, is what this is.

3 W. Foster, *The Embassy of Sir Thomas Roe to India, 1615–19, as Narrated in His Journal and Correspondence* (Oxford, 1926), pp. 280–1. The book was first published in 1899, which is another example of additional information not crucial to the main narrative.

4 D. Price, *Memoirs of the Emperor Jahanguier, Written by Himself; and Translated from a Persian Manuscript, by Major David Price* (London, 1829), p. 100.

5 Price, *Memoirs*, p. 104. This, of course, is the same book as in the previous note. Many historians have used the abbreviation 'ibid.' in this situation, but for those of us who did not study Latin, that doesn't help much. I prefer to do what many historians do now, which is to give a more straightforward abbreviation, using the surname of author or editor, a shortened title, and the page number. However, just for variety, I will use ibid. once later on.

6 F. Bernier, *Travels in the Mogul Empire. Translated from the French by*

Irving Brock, 2 vols. (London, 1826), vol. 2, p. 28. This was originally published in French in 1670.

7 Jean-Baptiste Tavernier, *Travels in India by Jean-Baptiste Tavernier*, 2nd edition edited by William Crooke, preface by V. Ball (London, 1925), p. 55. This English translation was originally published in 1889. Along with claiming that Marco Polo witnessed the rope trick, the *Occult Review* (1905) also claimed that Tavernier 'speaks of it in terms which plainly denote his bewilderment' (p. 292). This, however, was also a mistake. No wonder there has been so much confusion with this legend.

8 J. Ovington, *A Voyage to Surat in the Year 1689* (Oxford, 1929), p. 153.

9 Ovington, *Voyage*, p. 153.

10 Marco Polo's travels had been available in English since Frampton's translation of 1579 (see N. M. Penzer, *The Most Noble and Famous Travels of Marco Polo together with the Travels of Nicolo de Conti Edited from the Elizabethan Translation of John Frampton* (London, 1929), but further editions only appeared in the nineteenth century (for example, H. Murray, *The Travels of Marco Polo* (Edinburgh, 1844), T. Wright, *The Travels of Marco Polo the Venetian* (London, 1854) and, of course, Yule, *Marco Polo*). Ibn Battuta's travels were first translated in 1829 (see note 2 above), Bernier's diary in 1826 (see note 6 above). Tavernier (see note 7 above) had been translated more than two hundred years previously, but his nineteenth-century editor pointed out that this had been inadequate, and so the text was practically unknown to English readers (Tavernier, *Travels*, p. viii). The memoirs of Emperor Jahangir were also published in 1829 (see note 4 above) and, as you know, these also gave accounts of inexplicable jugglers' feats, and contributed to the growing image in the nineteenth century.

11 *Illustrated London News*, 27 April 1861, p. 17. Unfortunately, there were no illustrations to accompany the story.

12 R. M. Burns, *The Great Debate on Miracles: Joseph Glanvill to David Hume* (London, 1981) pp. 10–11.

13 Wright, *Marco Polo*, p. 19.

14 Edward Said's *Orientalism* (London, 1978), which provoked much of this recent debate, dealt with the Middle East, but others have discussed these issues in relation to South Asia. For example: R. Inden, *Imagining India* (London, 1990), C. Breckenridge and P. van der Veer, *Orientalism and the Postcolonial Predicament: Perspectives on South Asia* (Philadelphia, 1993), A. Chatterjee, *Representations of India, 1740–1840: The Creation of India in the Colonial Imagination* (London, 1998), R. King, *Orientalism and Religion: Postcolonial Theory, India and the Mystic East* (London, 1999).

15 Philip Meadows Taylor, *Confessions of a Thug* (London, 1839).

16 The quotations come from Lata Mani, 'Contentious Traditions: The Debate on Sati in Colonial India', in Kumkum Sangani and Sundesh Vaid (eds), *Recasting Women: Essays in Colonial History* (New Delhi, 1989) pp. 88–126. Mani's argument, however, is considerably more sophisticated than the gross generalisation I am making here.

17 Crispin Bates, 'Human Sacrifice in Colonial Central India: Mythology, Representation and Resistance', to be published in C. Bates (ed.), *Beyond Representation: constructions of identity in colonial and postcolonial India* (forthcoming). Crispin would no doubt want me to stress that it was much more complicated than these simplistic assertions of mine suggest. I would argue, in response, that my purpose is only to give the reader a flavour of the period, and that there is no claim to fully represent such a complex series of events in one sentence. He might reply that he accepted this, yet would repeat the need for some form of disclaimer, and remind me that, since the paper is not yet published, I need his permission to cite it. I would point out that this is the disclaimer, and then buy him a drink. All of this, however, is hypothetical, since he is

currently in Japan, so has no idea what I am up to. I will, however, buy him a drink when he gets back.

18 *Leisure Hour*, 1853, p. 794. The page number may give the impression that this was an enormous magazine. But that is because it relates to a bound volume of many issues. Other references give the date and a much smaller number, such as the one coming up next. In either case, however, the information should be sufficient for you to find the right page.

19 *Saturday Magazine*, 28 July 1832, p. 3.

20 *Leisure Hour*, 1853, pp. 791–4. *Chambers' Edinburgh Journal*, 16 March 1839, p. 69, had described the basic method but noted it was still unclear as to how it could actually work.

21 This was cited in *Spiritual Magazine*, 6, 1871, p. 59.

22 *The Oriental Annual, or Scenes in India; comprising twenty-five engravings from original drawings by William Daniell, RA, and a descriptive account by the Rev. Hobart Caunter* (London, 1834), pp. 25–7.

23 *Chambers' Edinburgh Journal*, 16 March 1839, p. 69.

24 *Family Herald*, 13, 1855, pp. 349–59; *All the Year Round*, 19 April 1862, p. 133; *Once a Week*, 4, 5 January 1861, pp. 40–3; *Spiritual Magazine*, 6, 1865, p. 120; T. Frost, *Lives of the Conjurors* (London, 1876), p. 114.

25 James Braid, *Magic, Witchcraft, Animal Magnetism, Hypnotism and Electro-biology* (London, 1852), p. 9. It was later claimed, once again without any evidence, that the Indian rope trick 'was performed for the first time before Maharaja Ranjit Singh, the Lion of the Punjab at Lahore in the presence of a British general and nobody could fathom its mystery. A second Exhibition was held in the city of Madras by another Magician' (*Cigam*, 1, 1954, no page number given, but the article appears in issue 3, February (from the Douglas Cameron collection). The author most likely got confused with the report of the live burial.

26 Braid, *Magic*, p. 14.

27 *Leisure Hour*, 1853, pp. 791–4.

28 *Family Herald*, 13, 1855, pp. 349–59. Others subsequently ruled out any form of deception, such as Col. H. S. Olcott, *People from the Other World* (London, 1875), p. 38.

29 *Fraser's Magazine*, 71, 1865, p. 35; see also *Fraser's Magazine*, 4, 1871, p. 515.

30 Religious Tract Society, *Magic, Pretended Miracles*, c.1850, p. 19. No publication date appears on this pamphlet, hence the guess.

31 *Penny Magazine*, 1833 (cutting from the Lane collection). This is a small cutting from a private collection, and does not give the date (other than the year) or page number.

32 *All the Year Round*, 11 February 1865, pp. 57–60.

33 *Chambers' Edinburgh Journal*, 28 November 1835, pp. 350–1.

34 'The Fakirs of India', n.d. (Lane collection). There is no information on this cutting at all, but the content, and the other cuttings around it, suggest it must have been late nineteenth-century.

Chapter 2

1 P. Spear, *A History of India*, vol. 2 (Harmondsworth, 1986), p. 131.

2 *Abracadabra*, 13 January 1973, pp. 42–4, 125–6; C. Waller, *Magical Nights at the Theatre* (Melbourne, 1980), pp. 8–9; D. Price, *Magic: A Pictorial History of Conjurers in the Theater* (New York, 1985), p. 142.

3 Heathcote Williams, *What Larks! Charles Dickens, Conjuror* (London, 1995); see also S. Tigner, 'Charles Dickens in and about Magic', *Journal of Magic History*, 1, 1979, pp. 88–110.

4 E. Dawes, *Stodare: The Enigma Variations* (Silver Spring, 1998), p. 48.

5 Dawes, *Stodare*, p. 82.

6 S. W. Clarke, *The Annals of Conjuring* (New York, 1983), p. 186. The Fakirs of Ava and Oolu were followed by the Fakir of Vishnu, and by fakirs of equally dubious Indian town-names. There was, for example, the Chicagoan Hindoo Rajah, as the *Chicago Sunday*

Examiner called him, who billed himself as Tomasha Walla, and whose parents had named him Edwin. He had offered to accompany a group of Hindus to America and, in the process, had learned both Hindustani and some juggling tricks. Later, in London, a serendipitous event occurred. 'I was feeling restless, and wandered down to the East India docks. There I met three of the most wretched looking individuals I have ever seen. They were Hindoo jugglers . . . I took them to a restaurant, fed them, gave them some decent clothes and persuaded them to come to the United States with me.' The philanthropist in Edwin was soon replaced by the manager and, on returning home, he arranged some bookings for 'my boys'. The first engagement, however, did not go as planned. 'My chief juggler, the sheikh,' Edwin explained, 'turned up missing. He had been drinking. I couldn't afford to let the chance slip, and on the spur of the moment I put on his costume, darkened my skin, and played his part. Every trick was worked perfectly.' So began his career as a touring Indian juggler which, exotic as it must have been, cannot have offered the prospects he desired. A few years later, Edwin had given it all up for a career in advertising, where his ability to deceive appears to have been better rewarded (*Chicago Sunday Examiner*, 24 November 1907).

7 Clarke, *Annals*, p. 283.

8 W. Hazlitt, 'The Indian Jugglers', *Table Talk* (London, 1821), pp. 77–89.

9 E. A. Dawes, *The Great Illusionists* (Seacaucus, N. J., 1979), p. 170.

10 Clarke, *Annals*, p. 127; see also Lauro poster (Lane collection), which shows the position of the juggler when performing this feat.

11 Clarke, *Annals*, p. 286.

12 *The Times*, 18 April 1876, p. 10.

13 Colonel Stodare, *Stodare's Fly-notes; or, Conjuring Made Easy* (London, 1867), pp. 5–6. This was a general theme among Western conjurors at this time.

14 W. E. Robinson, *Spirit Slate Writing and Kindred Phenomena* (London, 1899).
15 E. W. Lane, *An Account of the Manners and Customs of the Modern Egyptians* (London, 1860), originally published in 1836. This book, written in dry prose and claiming a degree of objectivity that few would accept today, described an Egypt of bizarre and extraordinary people and took some interest in feats of magic. For its role as a contributor to the Orientalist discourse of the East as weird and wonderful, see Rana Kabbani, *Imperial Fictions: Europe's Myths of the Orient* (London, 1994), pp. 37ff.
16 W. Collins, *The Moonstone* (London, 1868), p. 265.
17 There were, of course, those who denied this. When E. W. Lane, author of *An Account of the Manners and Customs of the Modern Egyptians,* published a new translation of *The Arabian Nights*, he was praised for stressing the worth of the text as evidence for analysis of a people rather than as a tale (Kabbani, *Imperial Fictions*, p. 37). Yet, as Kabbani points out, his decision to choose such tales, as with his interest in Oriental magic, was not accidental. Even those who dismissed romantic notions of the East nevertheless bought into the notion of an East associated with magic and mystery.

Chapter 3

1 *Chambers' Edinburgh Journal*, 21 May 1853, p. 321. The message was communicated via the medium Mrs Hayden, the first of several American mediums to ply their trade in Britain.
2 Clarke, *Annals*, pp. 199ff.
3 Geoffrey Lamb, *Victorian Magic* (London, 1976), p. 56.
4 *Spiritual Magazine*, 6, 1865, p. 89.
5 *Spiritual Magazine*, 6, 1865, p. 167.
6 *Spiritual Magazine*, 5, 1864, p. 524.

7 *Spiritual Magazine*, 6, 1865, p. 120.

8 Jean Burton, *Hey-day of a Wizard* (London, 1948), pp. 79–83.

9 P. Lamont, 'Conjuring Spirits and Conjuring Tricks', paper presented at the European Social Science History Conference, The Hague, 2002.

10 P. Lamont, 'Conjuring Up Images of India', paper presented at the Parapsychological Association Annual Convention, New York, 2001.

11 The *Observer* and the *Examiner* were cited in *Spiritual Magazine*, 6, 1871, pp. 550–2.

12 These quotations come from, respectively, the *Illustrated London News*, 27 April 1861, p. 17; *Family Herald*, 13, 1855, pp. 39–50; and *Chambers' Edinburgh Journal* (hereafter Chambers' Journal), 16 March 1839, p. 69.

13 This quotation appeared in an article in the *North American Review* in January 1893, written by the American magician, Harry Kellar, and was repeated in the *Journal of the Society for Psychical Research* (*JSPR*), 9, 1894, p. 354.

14 John Nevil Maskelyne, 'Oriental Jugglery', *Leisure Hour*, 1878, pp. 250–3, 298–301. The basket trick had already been 'exposed' in the *Popular Recreator*, 1873, pp. 145–6. The anonymous author had declared, 'We entirely disbelieve all the wonderful tales told of the Indian jugglers, the more so as in the few instances which we have at some pains really investigated, we have found them to be merely ordinary conjuring tricks, certainly skilfully done, but by no means on a par with those of the best European conjurors.' The author had also got the method wrong.

15 *Chambers' Journal*, 1901, p. 758. The article, 'Indian Conjuring Explained', was written by Professor Hoffmann, author of *Modern Magic* and other important conjuring texts.

16 See, respectively: *Chambers' Journal*, 1901, pp. 757–61; *New Penny Magazine*, 26 May 1900 (from the Lane collection, page nos unknown); *Scientific American*, 26 December 1914.

17 H. J. Burlinghame, *Around the World with a Magician and a Juggler* (Chicago, 1891), p. 183.

18 See, respectively: H. J. Burlinghame, *Leaves from a Conjurer's Scrap Books; or Modern Magicians and Their Works* (Chicago, 1891); S. S. Baldwin, *The Secrets of Mahatma Land Explained* (New York, 1895); C. Bertram, *Isn't It Wonderful?* (London, 1899).

19 Alongside the sceptical articles that sought to expose the methods of Indian juggling, many articles also appeared that failed to explain how the feats were done. For example: *Routledge's Every Boy's Annual Magazine*, January 1879, pp. 46–8; *Graphic*, 14 April 1888, pp. 393–4; *Graphic*, 2 January 1892, p. 13; *Boy's Own Paper*, 16, 1894, pp. 741–2; 'Oriental Magic' (*c.*1899, from the Devant collection); *Cassell's Family Magazine*, 15 July 1901 (Lane collection).

20 Josephine Ransom, *A Short History of the Theosophical Society* (Madras, 1938), pp. 27–34.

21 The letter is cited in J. N. Maskelyne, *The Fraud of Modern Theosophy Exposed: A Brief History of the Greatest Imposture ever perpetrated under the Cloak of Religion* (London, 1913), p. 29.

22 This is discussed more intelligently by Alex Owen, *The Darkened Room: Women, Power and Spiritualism in Late Victorian England* (London, 1989).

23 Muller quoted in J. Oppenheim, *The Other World: Spiritualism and Psychical Research, 1850–1914* (Cambridge, 1988), pp. 163–4.

24 Oppenheim, *Other World*, p. 185.

25 Stainton Moses in *Human Nature*, 11, 1877, p. 425.

26 See H. P. Blavatsky, *Isis Unveiled: A Master Key to the Mysteries of Ancient and Modern Science and Theology* (New York, 1877), vol. 1, p. 115 and vol. 2, p. 104.

27 S. Cranston, *HPB: The Extraordinary Life and Influence of Helena Blavatsky, Founder of the Theosophical Movement* (New York, 1993), p. 223.

28 *Proceedings on the Society for Physical Research (PSPR)*, 9, 1885, p. 205.

29 *PSPR*, 9, 1885, p. 207.

30 L. A. Weatherley and J. N. Maskelyne, *The Supernatural?* (Bristol, 1891), p. 215.

31 *Strand Magazine*, 18, 1899, pp. 657–64.

Chapter 4

1   J. Tebbel, *The Compact History of the American Newspaper* (New York, 1963), p. 130.

2   Lloyd Wendt, *The Rise of a Great American Newspaper* (Chicago, 1979), p. 119.

3   Wendt, *American Newspaper*, p. 113.

4   Wendt, *American Newspaper*, p. 121. The role of Medill and the *Tribune* in securing Lincoln's nomination for the presidency was later acknowledged in the *Dictionary of American Biography*, vol. 12 (London, 1933), p. 491.

5   Frederick W. Seward, *Seward at Washington as Senator and Secretary of State: A Memoir of His Life with a Selection of His Letters* (New York, 1891), p. 277.

6   Humbert S. Nelli, *Business of Crime: Italians and Syndicate Crime in the United States* (New York, 1976), p. 127.

7   Frederic Bancroft, *The Life of William H. Seward*, 2 vols (New York, 1900), vol. 2, pp. 521–3.

8   Bancroft, *Life of Seward*, pp. 474–5.

9   Tebbel, *Compact History*, p. 118.

10 Nelli, *Business of Crime*, p. 111.

11 Wendt, *American Newspaper*, p. 270.

12 *The World's Greatest Newspaper. A handbook of newspaper administration . . . minutely depicting, in word and picture, 'how it's done' by the world's greatest newspaper* (Chicago, 1922), p. 45.

13 *World's Greatest Newspaper*, pp. 45–6.

14 Wendt, *American Newspaper*, p. 270.

15 Tebbel, *Compact History*, pp. 156–7.

16 *World's Greatest Newspaper*, pp. 45–6.

17 P. Kinsley, *The Chicago Tribune: Its First Hundred Years, 1880–1900*, vol. 3 (Chicago, 1946), p. 135.

18 *Chicago Daily Tribune*, 8 August 1890, p. 16.

19 The *Tribune* was published in two parts, and p. 16 was the front page of the second part.

20 Weatherley and Maskelyne, *Supernatural?*, p. 161). According to the British journal *Photography* (18 December 1890), the story was within weeks 'going the round of the [British] provincial press'.

21 *Chicago Daily Tribune*, 6 December 1890.

22 *People's Friend*, 1891, pp. 70–1.

23 Ibid. (see note 5, Chapter 1).

24 Weatherley and Maskelyne, *Supernatural?*, pp. 161–2.

25 *JSPR*, 5, 1891, pp. 84–6.

26 This translation is from Yule, *Marco Polo*, vol. 1, p. 308.

27 Yule, *Marco Polo*, vol. 1, pp. 308–11.

28 In 1878, Maskelyne described the chain trick as a feat of Chinese jugglers (*Leisure Hour*, 1878, pp. 250–3). By 1891, however, he correctly attributed the story to Jahangir (Weatherley and Maskelyne, *Supernatural?*, p. 165).

29 Olcott, *Other World*, pp. 328–32.

30 *Light*, 4 April 1891, p. 182; *Psychische Studien*, 18, 1891, pp. 342–5, 411–21; Alfred Lehmann, 1896 (cited in Poul Tuxen and Else Pauly, *The Parable of the Climbing Juggler* (Copenhagen, 1953), p. 353.

31 *PSPR*, 4, 1887, pp. 411–12

32 *PSPR*, 9, 1894, pp. 354–66.

33 Harry Kellar, *A Magician's Tour: Up and Down and Round About the Earth, Being the Life and Adventures of the American Nostradamus, Harry Kellar. Edited by His Faithful 'Familia', 'Satan Junior'* (Chicago, 1886), p. 80.

34 *JSPR*, 4, 1889, p. 107.

35 *Graphic*, 2 January 1892, p. 13.

36 *Boy's Own Paper*, 16 August 1894, p. 742.

37 *Chicago Sunday Examiner*, 7 April 1907 (Lane collection, no page number given).

Chapter 5

1 *JSPR*, 11, 1904, p. 300.

2 S. T. Burchett's account was not the first to appear. There had been the occasional story in the popular press (*Titbits*, 30 March 1901; *Pearson's Weekly*, 1901, n.d. (Lane collection)). However, Burchett was the first to put his name to his account, and this made it qualitatively more plausible. It also appeared in a scientific journal, lending greater credence to the account

3 *Magazine of Magic*, 16 September 1916, p. 62.

4 Gibson later stated that 'group hypnotism of this sort would be beyond the power of any man' (W. Gibson, *The Book of Secrets: Miracles Ancient and Modern*, 1927, p. 73).

5 The letters were published in the *Daily Mail* throughout January 1919.

6 *Magic Circular*, 12, 1918, pp. 85–7.

7 Lieutenant Holmes announced that he had taken the photograph in a letter to the *Daily Mail* in January. It was published later in the *Strand Magazine*, 57, 1919, p. 311.

8 *Daily Mail*, 28 January 1919.

9 *Magic Circular*, 13, 1919, p. 73.

10 *Magic Circular*, 13, 1919, p. 86.

11 *Daily Mail*, 28 January 1919.

12 R. H. Elliot, *The Myth of the Mystic East* (Edinburgh, 1934), p. 96.

13 *Magic Circular*, 13, 1919, p. 87.

Chapter 6

1 *Era*, 27 May 1922.
2 C. Hertz, *A Modern Mystery Merchant: The Trials, Tricks and Travels of Carl Hertz* (London, 1924), p. 167.
3 Major L. H. Branson, *Indian Conjuring* (London, 1922), p. 87.
4 P. C. Sorcar, *Indian Magic* (Delhi, 1970), pp. 60–1.
5 H. Goldin, *It's Fun to Be Fooled* (London, 1952), pp. 166–7.
6 A representation of Thurston's poster advertising the rope trick can be found in John Fisher, *Paul Daniels and the Story of Magic* (London, 1987), p. 12.
7 The letter, published in the *Civil and Military Gazette*, 4 October 1926, was reprinted in the *Magic Circular*, 19, 1925, pp. 76–8.
8 Minutes of the Occult Committee of the Magic Circle, 19 July 1933.
9 *Magic Circular*, 19, 1925, pp. 77–8.
10 T. Secrett, *Twenty-five Years with Earl Haig* (London, 1929), pp. 43–60.

Chapter 7

1 Elliot's views can be seen in Elliot, *Mystic East*, pp. 117, 133.
2 Minutes, Occult Committee, 19 July 1933. A similarly brief synopsis is given in Elliot, *Mystic East*, pp. 97–9
3 Elliot, *Mystic East*, p. 88.
4 E. A. Dawes, 'Lieutenant-Colonel R. H. Elliot and "the Myth of the Mystic East"', *Magic Circular*, 89, 1995, pp. 177–9.
5 Elliot, *Mystic East*, pp. 87–8.
6 The announcement was made in the *Magic Circular*, 28, 1934, p. 108.
7 *Magic Circular*, 28, 1934, p. 144.
8 *Magic Circular*, 28, 1934, pp. 162–3.
9 *Magic Circular*, 28, 1934, p. 136.

10 *Magic Circular*, 28, 1934, p. 181.

11 Hertz, *Modern Mystery Merchant*, p. 167.

12 Branson, *Indian Conjuring*, preface.

13 *Magic Circular*, 28, 1934, pp. 136–8.

14 Occult Committee Minutes, 11 May 1934.

15 *Magic Circular*, 28, 1934, pp. 136–8.

16 Occult Committee Minutes, 9 June 1934.

17 Occult Committee Minutes, 9 June 1934.

18 *Chambers' Journal*, 3, 1934, pp. 923–8.

19 The exchange of letters was published in the *Listener*, throughout December 1934 and January 1935.

20 *Daily Telegraph*, 5 and 8 May 1934.

21 *Listener*, 16 May 1934, p. 843.

22 *Listener*, 5 December 1934, p. 959.

23 *Listener*, 12 December 1934, p. 998.

24 The relevant letters were published in the *Listener* throughout January and February 1935.

25 *Listener*, 13 February 1935; *Magic Circular*, 28, 1934, p. 98.

26 *Listener*, 13 February 1995.

27 Quotations from letters in the *Listener*, 20 February 1935.

28 *Listener*, 16 January 1935; H. Price, *Confessions of a Ghost-hunter* (London, 1935), pp. 344ff.

29 BBC internal letter (Harry Price collection).

30 *Listener*, 16 January 1935.

31 *Listener*, 13 February 1935.

32 Don Wilkie, *American Secret Service Agent* (New York, 1934), pp. 13–14. The author was Wilkie's son, who also joined the Service.

33 Unknown newspaper source dated 15 December 1934 (US Secret Service Archive).

34 *True Detective Magazine*, October 1941 (US Secret Service Archive).

35 This was claimed in the *Montreal Star*. Whether it was true or not is difficult to confirm, since the original has since disappeared from

Secret Service files (Rhodri Jeffreys-Jones, *Cloak and Dollar: A History of American Secret Intelligence* (New Haven, 2001), p. 41).

36 Unknown newspaper source dated January 1911 (US Secret Service Archive); David R. Johnson, *Illegal Tender: Counterfeiting and the Secret Service in Nineteenth-century America* (Washington, 1995), pp. 178–9.

37 Jeffreys-Jones, *Cloak and Dollar*, p. 57.

38 Wilkie, *American Secret Service Agent*, p. 174

39 Wilkie, *American Secret Service Agent*, pp. 14–15.

40 *True Detective Magazine*, c.1937 (US Secret Service Archive).

41 Wilkie, *American Secret Service Agent*, pp. 27–8.

Chapter 8

1 Rupert T. Gould, *The Stargazer Talks* (London, 1943), pp. 7–13.

2 W. H. Russell, *The Prince of Wales's Tour: A Diary in India* (London, 1877), p. ix.

3 Russell, *Diary*, p. 332

4 Hertz, *Modern Mystery Merchant*, p. 167.

5 Lee Siegel, *Net of Magic: Wonders and Deceptions in India* (Chicago, 1991), p. 201.

6 E. Moulton, *Lord Northbrook's Indian Administration, 1872–1876* (London, 1968).

7 Frost, *Conjurors*; J. N. Maskelyne, *Modern Spiritualism: A Short Account of its Rise and Progress, with Some Exposures of So-Called Spirit Media* (London, 1876); Maskelyne, 'Oriental Jugglers'.

8 L. Jacolliot, *Occult Science in India and among the Ancients* (London, 1919), p. iv, originally published in 1884.

9 *Graphic*, 14 April 1888, p. 394.

10 In an essay on Indian juggling, Clarke had referred to the rope trick, and had pointed out that Lord Lonsdale had offered a reward of ten thousand pounds. This had been in 1902, by which time the

then Prince of Wales had also visited India, and Clarke noted that 'great efforts were made to show him the best of native tricks'. This is probably where the confusion came from. A more careful reading of Clarke's writing would have shown that he did not believe that the story had been known for very long. He rightly pointed out that there were older stories that were not from India, such as Ibn Battuta's Chinese thong trick, but he also noted that they were 'not generally known till about the middle of the last century', and that the Indian rope trick had only attracted attention from about 1890 (Clarke, *Annals*, pp. 126–7).

11 Hertz seems to have made the original error, and this was then inadvertently copied by: O. Fischer, *Illustrated Magic* (New York, 1931), p. 187; D. H. Rawcliffe, *The Psychology of the Occult* (New York, 1959), p. 299; Siegel, *Net of Magic*, p. 201; Brian W. Haines, 'The Indian Rope Trick', *Skeptic*, 8, 1995, pp. 17–19; and, most recently, Booth, *Extending Magic*, p. 216.

12 *Magic Circular*, 13, 1919, p. 125.

13 Elliot, *Blackwood's Magazine*, 237, 1935, p. 445; the magician Paul Curry also claimed that the legend started in China (Paul Curry, *Magician's Magic* (London, 1965), p. 79).

14 H. L. Varma, *The Indian Rope Trick* (Bombay, 1942), p. 52.

15 Varma, *Indian Rope Trick*, p. 69.

16 Varma, *Indian Rope Trick*, p. 77. This translation is confirmed in George Thibaut, *The Vedanta Sutras* (Oxford, 1890), p. 70.

17 Varma, *Indian Rope Trick*, p. 13. When Radhakrishnan later discussed the same sutra, he made no reference to the rope trick (S. Radhakrishnan, *The Brahmasutra: The Philosophy of Spiritual Life* (London, 1960), pp. 69–70). The earliest reference I have been able to find that compares the sutra to the rope trick is not until 1951 (Helmuth von Glasenapp, *Die Philosophie der Inder* (Stuttgart, 1985), p. 191).

18 The earliest English translation of this is Manilal N. Dvivedi,

Mandukyopanishad (Bombay, 1894), pp. 18–19, though he does not refer to the Indian rope trick. Neither does the next translation, S. Nikhilananda, *The Mandukyopanishad with Gaudapada's Karika and Sankara's Commentary* (Mysore, 1936), pp. 44–6. An explicit link between Sankara's reference and the Indian rope trick was made much later, however, by: Tuxen and Pauly, *Climbing Juggler*, p. 355; T. M. P. Mahadevan, *Gaudapada: A Study in Early Advaita* (Madras, 1960), pp. 105–6; M. Eliade, *The Two and the One* (London, 1965); A. Sharma, *The Rope and the Snake: A Metaphorical Exploration of Advaita Vedanta* (New Delhi, 1997). E. Conze, *Buddhism: Its Essence and Development* (New York, 1955), also cites the rope trick as an example of maya, and refers to Ibn Battuta's Chinese thong trick (p. 174).

19 E. B. Cowell (ed.), *The Jataka, or Stories of the Buddha's Former Births*, vol. 4 (Cambridge, 1901), p. 204. It is worth pointing out that this story is not about a rope magically rising into the air, and does not mention anybody disappearing.

20 M. Eliade, *Shamanism: Archaic Techniques of Ecstasy* (London, 1989), pp. 50, 78, 136, 226. The book was written in 1946–51, and first published in English in 1964.

21 Eliade, *Two and the One*, p. 166.

22 In 1912, Felix Blei was told by Harry Lyons, manager of Harry Kellar, that he had invented the story to outdo the Davenports. This, it was claimed, had happened in Australia some years after his last trip to India with Kellar (Felix Blei, 'The Hindu Rope Trick', *Billboard*, 13 August 1927). A few years later, it was claimed that a magician called Dugwar, who was in Britain in 1877, suggested the method for the rope trick, but this claim was not made until 1919, and there is no contemporary support for it (*Magic Circular*, 13, 1919, pp. 125–9).

23 W. Gibson, *Secrets of the Great Magicians* (London, 1976), p. 80.

24 *To-day*, 10 September 1938.

25 A further example of an unsubstantiated claim can be found in

Will Durant's *Story of Civilization* (*Kulturgeschichte der Menschheit*, Bern, 1959), vol. 4, p. 245. The author claims that the rope trick can be found in Nicole Oresme's *Book of Divinacions*, originally published in 1382. However, Durant's description of the trick is vague, it does not refer to the trick being Indian, and I can find no such description in the English translation of Oresme's book (G. Coopland, *Nicole Oresme and the Astrologers: A Study of His Livre de Divinacions* (Liverpool, 1952)).

26 Playbill for Astley's, 1864, reads: 'Unparalleled and Enthusiastic Reception of Sig. Redmond Rival to the Brothers Davenport, who Nightly . . .' (www.dramatispersonae.com).

27 *The Great Wizard's Handbook of Magic, or Parlour Entertainment. Containing also, Fortune-telling by Cards, and the Rope Trick*, pamphlet, *c*.1880 (British Library).

28 There was, however, a reference to another rope trick having been performed in India, though it could hardly have been well known. John Henry Anderson, the self-styled Wizard of the North, and the most famous British conjuror in the mid-nineteenth century, printed an eye-witness account of another trick with 'a ball of twine, which [the juggler] appeared to toss into my lap, keeping hold of one end so that it unrolled the whole distance between him and me . . . yet, when I put my hand down to take it, and looked down for it, there was nothing there – *nothing was there* – and at the same instant I perceived the juggler balancing it on the end of his finger' (Professor Anderson, 'Indian Juggler and Magicians', *c*.1850 (Peter Lane collection)). The reference to the 'ball of twine' suggests a possible partial source of Kellar's later story; Kellar might have read Anderson's leaflet, but the fact that neither Anderson nor the witness mention '*the* Indian rope trick' further illustrates the lack of awareness of any such trick at this time.

29 They had appeared, after all, as a footnote to the section on China in Yule's *Marco Polo*; see pp. 76–77.

30 See note 28, chapter 4; and Maskelyne was by no means alone. The same mistake was made in 1880, when an English translation of old Chinese folk tales appeared, and one of those tales was of a rope being thrown into the air. The editor compared the tale to Jahangir's chain trick, but described it as a feat performed by Chinese jugglers, and made no reference to India whatsoever (Herbert A. Giles, *Strange Stories from a Chinese Studio* (Shanghai, 1936), p. 376, originally published in 1880). Yet another example of this error can be found in an unidentified newspaper article *c.*1899, entitled 'Oriental Magic' (Devant collection, cutting album VI, no. 5400).

31 Blavatsky did not make any reference to Sankara, even when she explained her 'Indian tape-climbing trick' in terms of maya, a concept typically associated with Sankara (Blavatsky, *Isis Unveiled*, vol. 1, pp. 472–4).

32 See, in particular, Sharma, *Rope and the Snake*, for numerous references on this topic.

33 This, in fact, is precisely what happened recently when I asked Paul Dundas, a Sanskrit scholar at the University of Edinburgh, to look at the relevant passage of Sankara's commentary in the original Sanskrit. When I asked whether there was any reference to a rope trick, his response related solely to the rope–snake metaphor.

34 Goldin, *Fun to Be Fooled*, pp. 166–7.

35 Magic Circular, 15, 1921, pp. 175–6.

36 Thurston, H. *My Life of Magic* (Baltimore, 1929), p. 192. The same point was made by Hertz, *Modern Mystery Merchant*, p. 163.

37 This comes from a St George's Hall leaflet, an original copy of which is in the Magic Circle library, but which is also reprinted in D. Devant, *My Magic Life* (London, 1931), pp. 130–1. Notably, Devant's stage version did begin with a dismembered man being restored to health (*Magic Circular*, 11, 1917, pp. 84ff.), but other stage versions at this time – by Hertz, Goldin, Le Roy – did not.

38 *Spectator*, 9 March 1934, p. 63.
39 Maskelyne's words, from the *Sunday Pictorial*, are cited in G. H. Rooke, 'Indian Occultism: The Rope-trick and Other Phenomena', paper presented to the East India Association, 1936.
40 Eliade's example of a ropeless rope trick is also represented in E. Burger and R. Neale, *Magic and Meaning* (Seattle, 1995), p. 55.
41 *To-day*, 10 September 1938, pp. 6–7.
42 Booth, *Extending Magic*, pp. 217–18.

Chapter 9

1 *Sunday Express*, 17 March 1935.
2 *Fate*, 17, 1964, p. 73. This article is, in effect, a truncated version of a chapter from Sorcar, *Indian Magic*.
3 *Occult Review*, 1905, p. 292.
4 *Edwards Monthly*, April 1909, p. 5
5 *Popular Science Siftings*, 10 December 1918, pp. 203–4.
6 Maskelyne, *Fraud of Modern Theosophy*, pp. 23–4.
7 Branson, *Indian Conjuring*, pp. 83–4. Branson's scepticism was shared by Hereward Carrington, the distinguished psychical researcher and amateur conjuror, who 'did not at all agree with Mr Maskelyne's explanation' (Hereward Carrington, *Hindu Magic: An Exposé of the Tricks of the Yogis and Fakirs of India* (Kansas City, 1913), p. 48).
8 Lord Frederic Hamilton, *Here, There and Everywhere* (London, 1921), pp. 39–42.
9 Elliot, *Mystic East*, p. 91.
10 See the recent biography of Hanussen: Mel Gordon, *Erik Jan Hanussen: Hitler's Jewish Clairvoyant* (Feral House, 2001).
11 H. Price, *Confessions of a Ghost Hunter* (London, 1936), pp. 351ff. A year later, a less sinister, though equally plausible, explanation was suggested by the satirist Robert Benchley. He explained that: 'the fakir has asked his audience to inhale and exhale deeply,

occasionally stopping breathing entirely for a space of perhaps ten or fifteen minutes . . . When his audience is in the proper state of oxygen poisoning, so that their eyes are nicely crossed . . . the fakir throws his rope up. In the meantime, a large cloud of smoke has been sent up from a nearby bonfire . . . [and] an accomplice has thrown a lasso to catch the top of the fakir's rope' (*Liberty*, 14 November 1931, pp. 40–1). A more serious explanation at this time was that the memory was the result of the witness having 'dozed off [and] dreamed the supposed facts' (*JSPR*, 25, 1929, p. 180).

12 Other trick rope theories that have been put forward include Fischer, *Illustrated Magic*, p. 187, and Gould, *Stargazer Talks*, p. 12, but none has been successful.

13 Sorcar, *Indian Magic*, pp. 66–7.

14 Joseph Dunninger in Sorcar, *Indian Magic*, p. 74.

15 *Sunday Express*, 17 March 1935, p. 15.

16 Gould, *Stargazer Talks*, p. 8.

17 M. Cramer, 'Indian Rope Trick', in P. Brookesmith (ed.), *Open Files* (London, 1984), p. 53.

18 *Sunday Express*, 17 March 1935, p. 15; Gould, *Stargazer Talks*, p. 8.

19 Professor Belzibub, 'Old Indian Magic', *Cigam*, 2, 1955, p. 124.

20 For all the problems with these gross generalisations, a range of areas could be identified – such as increased productivity, industrial growth, the introduction of social welfare programmes, the maintenance of a secular state, the increase in Western-style education, and the retention of English as an official language – which suggest that India, under Nehru, was becoming more like the modern West.

21 John Keel, *Visitors from Space: The Astonishing True Story of the Mothman Prophecies* (St Albans, 1976), p. 65

22 John Keel, *Jadoo* (New York, 1958), pp. 128–48.

23 Keel, *Jadoo*, p. 169.

24 Sorcar, *Indian Magic*, p. 78.

25 Siegel, *Net of Magic*, p. 208, suggests that Vadaramakrishna read Sorcar's account, but the chronology does not fit. Keel was reported performing his feat in 1955, and published Vadaramakrishna's explanation in 1957, whereas Sorcar's account was first published in 1960.

26 Sorcar, *Indian Magic*, pp. 73–7.

27 L. N. Das, *Indian Rope Trick in Ginger* (Calcutta, 1960)

28 Das, *Indian Rope Trick*, pp. 50–2.

29 *Fate*, 17, 1964, pp. 76–7; Cramer, 'Indian Rope Trick', p. 53; Reader's Digest, *How's It Done?* (London, 1990), pp. 400–1; and, at the time of writing, can be found on the Internet at: www.abc.net.au/science/k2/moments/s155947.htm

30 Siegel, *Net of Magic*, p. 208.

31 The quotation is from V. E. Fisher, *Introduction to Abnormal Psychology* (New York, 1932), and was later cited in Rawcliffe, *Psychology of the Occult*, p. 298. The *JSPR* also continues to debate the theory, at one point stating that 'it can hardly have had its origins in the narrative printed in 1890 in the *Chicago Tribune*' (*JSPR*, 24, 1928, p. 345). This was in reference to the collective hallucination theory, not the legend of the rope trick. On the contrary, the claim was repeated that the rope trick had been seen by Marco Polo.

32 David Tomory, *A Season in Heaven: True Tales from the Road to Kathmandu* (Melbourne, 1998), p. 196.

33 Andrija Puharich, *Uri: The Original and Authorised Biography of Uri Geller – the Man Who Baffles the Scientists* (London, 1974).

34 Andrija Puharich, *Beyond Telepathy* (London, 1974, pp. 33–4.

35 Ormond McGill, *The Mysticism and Magic of India* (London, 1977), p. 34.

36 *New Scientist*, 21 February 1998, pp. 32–3.

37 *New Scientist*, 12 April 1997, p. 13; *Daily Telegraph*, 28 March 1997.

38 Leonard H. Miller, *Thrilling Magic* (Bideford, 1984), p. 12, first published in 1959.

39 Joseph Ovette, *Miraculous Hindu Feats* (Oakland, 1947), p. 9.

40 Derek Lever, *Stranger than Fiction* (Bideford, 1978), p. 15, first published in 1961.

Chapter 10

1 *Chambers' Journal*, 3, 1934, p. 928.

2 *Blackwood's Magazine*, 237, 1935, p. 457.

3 Hamilton, *Here, There*, p. 40. Similar points were made in the *Magic Circular*, 15, 1921, p. 279; Gould, *Stargazer Talks*, p. 8

4 *Chambers' Journal*, 3, 1934, p. 928.

5 Maskelyne, *Fraud of Modern Theosophy*, p. 21.

6 *Spectator*, 9 March 1934, p. 364.

7 Varma, *Indian Rope Trick*, p. 113.

8 *Daily Mail*, 28 January 1919.

9 *Magic Circular*, 15, 1921, p. 248.

10 Richard Wiseman and Peter Lamont, 'Unravelling the Rope Trick', *Nature*, 383, 1996, pp. 212–13.

11 *All the Year Round*, 19 April 1862, p. 133.

12 *Daily Telegraph*, 16 June 1932.

13 Fischer, *Illustrated Magic*, p. 187.

Epilogue

1 The actual name of the guest house was Green Villa, run by my friend, Raju. When I told Raju his place would get a mention in my book, he immediately demanded 10 per cent of royalties. I told him that, as he was too expensive, I would use a fictitious name. For the same reason, I have avoided using Raju's name and, following an afternoon of intense negotiation, have opted for the

name of Raju's son, Sooraj. My lawyers wish to make it clear that this in no way indicates a willingness to donate 10 per cent of royalties to Sooraj or any of Raju's family. However, I can thoroughly recommend Green Villa Guest House.

2   This framed cutting sat on the desk of Companion Travel Agency, Thiruvananthapuram, Kerala.

3   *Hindu*, 11 December 2001.

INDEX

Index

CREDITS

P. 10 the *Graphic*; p. 19 *Saturday Magazine*; p. 33 reproduced in E. A. Dawes, *The Great Illusionists*; p. 35 *Magic Wand*; p. 45 Maskelyne: Topham; p. 45 lock photographed courtesy of the Magic Circle; p. 59 *Strand Magazine*; p. 62 Hulton Getty; p. 83 *Chicago Daily Tribune*; p. 104 *Strand Magazine*/Peter Lane Collection; p. 110 reproduced in *Magazine of Magic*; p. 114 reproduced in *Magazine of Magic*; p. 121 *The Magic Circular*; p. 141 Harry Price Collection; p. 143 Harry Price Collection; p. 146 Library of Congress/Waldon Fawcett; p. 162 *Punch*; p. 171 *Sunday Graphic and Sunday News*; p. 186 Aldus Archive; p. 188 *Magic Wand*; p. 207 Peter Lane Collection; p. 209 Kobal Collection.